Guerrilla Gardening for Long-Term Survival

by Fred Demara

Paladin Press, First Edition

Ogden Publications, Revised Edition © 2019
ISBN: 978-0-941678-01-8

Publisher: Bill Uhler
Editorial Director: Oscar H. Will III
Merchandise and Event Director: Andrew Perkins
Production Director: Bob Cucciniello
Special Content Editorial Director: Christian Williams
Special Content Group Editor: Jean Teller
Special Content Assistant Editor: Haleigh McGavock
Book Design and Layout: Karen Rooman

All photos courtesy Pixabay and Getty Images unless otherwise noted.

1503 S.W. 42nd St.
Topeka, KS 66609, USA
Telephone (785) 274-4300
Fax (785) 274-4305
www.ogdenpubs.com

Printed in the U.S.A

Table of Contents

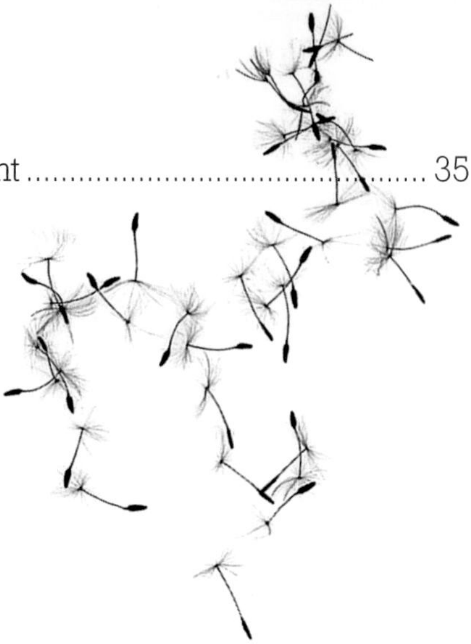

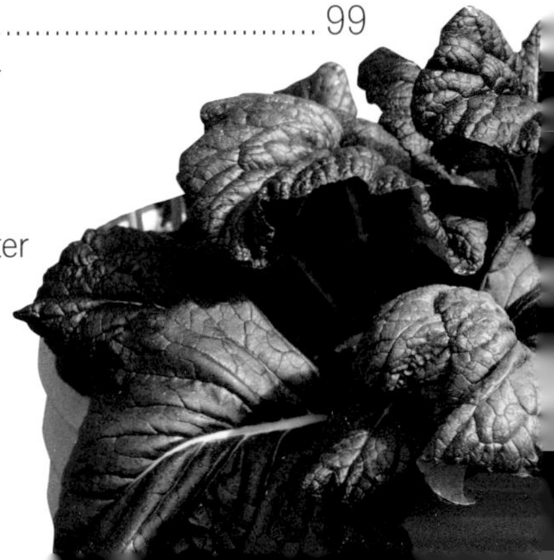

Table of Contents

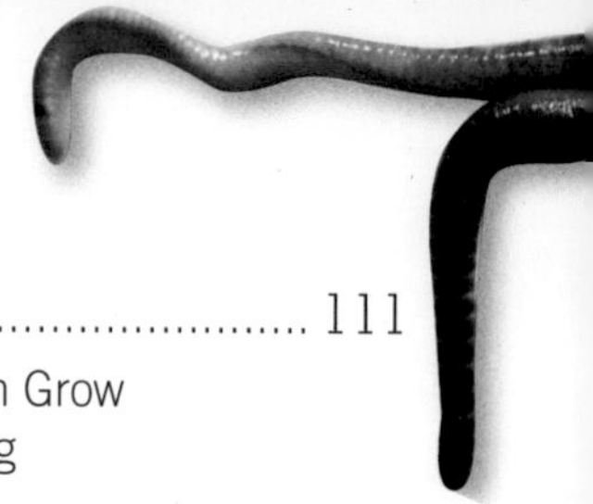

Gooseberrries

Preface

Springing as we do from an agrarian society with a tradition of self-reliance, the thought that it might be officially discouraged, or even illegal, to grow your own food is a preposterous idea. But it is no longer unthinkable. Controlling the food supply is viewed in some quarters as a means to control the populace.

Victory Gardens, U.S. Department of Agriculture (USDA) instructional booklets, and county extension agents are being replaced by the electronic benefit transfer (EBT) card for buying factory food you never earned. And you'd better toe the mark.

The premise that at some point this inherently unsustainable system implodes and you will have to feed yourself appears to be almost an eventuality. The potential for starving wannabe hunter-gathers with an eye for your food resources makes secrecy an inherent aspect of your own food-growing sufficiency. Planting for privacy has thus become an unfortunate consideration in your plans of planting for survival.

Lotus seed pod

Chapter 1

Reaping Begins with Sowing

Chapter 1

Taro leaves and flower

STARTING WITH THE GARDEN OF EDEN, agriculture has never been easy. It has always been a gamble and has always been labor intensive, but it has proven the surest way to a full belly. Folks interested in self-sufficiency, including the old-timers who didn't have any other options, found early on that there was considerable advantage to growing those foods you previously sought in the wild as a hunter-gatherer. A crop can be nurtured, controlled, or even protected as need be. Today, self-provisioning is an important skill set that provides one more useful implement in a doomsday scenario toolbox. It can be a primary or supplemental source of nutrition: It takes a lot of food for an active person to survive.

There is a synergism and efficiency to working the soil in cooperation with others, but most of the low-level subsistence agriculture explored here is readily done alone and in a variety of situations, with nature your only partner. The very concept of planting, nurturing, and harvesting implies a venue to do them, and that you will be in one spot long enough to do so.

But not necessarily: Even as a semi-nomad, you can plant many crops and revisit them for tending or harvesting. Some quick-turnaround crops can even be grown on your back as you keep moving (see Chapter 11). A truly nomadic lifestyle often will be impractical in tumultuous times, but fluid movement between viable resources may be a necessity.

The phrase "guerrilla gardening" implies discreet, subrosa, or even secret and small-scale agriculture in a setting where the grower doesn't want anyone to know of his crops. The reasons in a worst-case scenario would be that food resources have assumed their predictable and crucial importance when there is no outside source. In any instance where there is a general breakdown of society, everybody will still have to eat. Food is likely to be regarded as wealth worth stealing or used as a means of population control. If you have your own food, you have a better chance of having your own liberty as well.

The picture painted here inescapably hints at considerations of clandestine agriculture that are a reality to outlaws who have over the years grown crops that are in themselves contraband and must be hidden—from authorities, thieves, competitors, and vermin. This study has no particular interest in crops aside from those that provide human nutrition, but many of the experiences of those clandestine agriculturists apply even to this discussion where wholesome nutrition is the only rationale. Because when no food is available, or growing your own food becomes illegal or dangerous, being able to grow your own—and keep it your own—will be invaluable.

Jerusalem Artichoke and root

Chapter 1

Thorny Blackberry Vine

No tools? No till? No time? No problem!

Jungle dwellers in low-population areas often employ plant-and-revisit techniques for native or naturalized crops that are well adapted to being ignored after planting merely as a way to most efficiently use the resources they have. Even most domesticated food plants do not require fields as such. Crops indigenous to the area that need only to be given a leg up at their early stages to get established can thus be the prime candidates for plant-and-visit farming. The economy of scale will be replaced by the safety of diversity—diverse crops in diverse but accessible locations.

A poster child for this might be taro, which has traveled worldwide from Southeast Asia to become a starchy staple of Polynesia. It is now grown or planted in appropriate settings and can be pretty much ignored until harvest, although it has become a large commercial crop as well.

A North American or temperate-region counterpart to taro would be the Jerusalem artichoke, actually a wild sunflower with a large tuber that keeps on growing until you dig it up in the fall, the next year, or even the year after that. Sunflowers per se also make a good no-tend crop if you can compete with birds and rodents, and the seeds or seed heads keep well.

Consider where you are and what food staples do well there and ponder whether a particular crop might do well "in the wild." I had a good friend who spent a couple of years behind Japanese lines in Burma and learned from the Kachins how to eat locally. Aside from all the usual suspects of strange edible plants and bugs, he was surprised to find potatoes—as in what resembled small russets—growing wild in the Burmese jungle. The locals had a name for them, and they always regarded them as native plants. "Everybody" knows that spuds like cool nights, a rare thing in Burma, but there they were. He had no luck convincing his friends that the spuds somehow had migrated from South America. But, then, he had no luck convincing them there was a South America either.

The point here is to think expansively when considering a crop that will do well in your venue, even when planted and left on its own, or that may readily go feral. All plants were at one time wild, although you can expect many to revert to original characteristics when not nurtured. Both annuals and perennials are worth considering. Some of the most common feral food plants around abandoned American settlements are garlic, top onions, rhubarb, ground cherries, and all the common fruit trees but, depending on your location, can include the whole spectrum of heirloom plantings. A plant being considered as a plant-and-revisit crop gets extra points, of course, if it happens to be something that a marauding forager might not recognize or local animals would not molest.

If you project that you will be in a static location before, during, and after whatever upheaval you imagine, the core plants of either circuit-rider plantings or a mini-homestead hidey hole could well be mostly perennials. Fruits, nuts, and berries are all viable staples, which usually require much less tending, and many are preferable for storability and shelf life. If you have to leave your digs due to unforeseen circumstances, remember that Johnny Appleseed probably died with a happy heart, knowing he had left a legacy of feeding others he would never meet.

Few perennials give a quick return compared to annuals, but the investment in time gives a greater and more extended payback. As always when planting perennials, develop a plan. The plan should not only include the obvious—such as compatibility with other plants and juxtaposition so this one does not starve that one for nutrients and sunlight—but also that the overall presentation does not look like domestic trees and shrubs planted on purpose. This way, different plantings can protect one another from weather, sight, browsers, or marauders. It's hard to go wrong with thorny blackberry vines as a perimeter bramble, as this alone will often keep casual observers from getting close enough to see.

The type of consideration will vary with your climate and situation, but not planting vines where they can choke fruit trees and keeping walnut trees away from plants sensitive to the juglone they produce are the sort of things to think about, as are such points as avoiding plants that harbor insects or diseases that will affect other crops. Study individually what you are considering planting together, because there can be a synergism, as well as an antipathy, between certain plants. Remember that, of course, you can often use the shelter of an established perennial plot to harbor many annuals or biennials.

Forest Gardening, "Food Forests," and Permaculture

These terms, not really interchangeable but sometimes used interchangeably, do embrace overlapping principles. They share the idea that nature only does what works in the long run, and that mimicking the way nature grows plants is, in the long run, our best idea. Although it may be hard to imagine feeding an entire planet in this manner with macro applications, there are principles within these lines of thought that are universally beneficial. And in microcosm, for feeding oneself, efficiently and discreetly, the benefits are obvious and many.

One notable feature is that because this kind of agriculture copies nature, it thus tends to look like nature. A survival garden with carefully manicured rows of veggies looks like a food source to marauders and is far more likely to be prospected and raided. A further benefit of these "food forests" is the synergism between plants, if they are carefully selected for compatibility. Think of the "three sisters" Native American technique of planting corn, beans, and squash together so the corn provides a trellis for the beans, and the squash

Robert Hart's system used multiple tiers, copying the distinct levels of a natural forest. The difference is that here everything growing is useful to the person who planted it. Hart naturally favored shade-tolerant perennial vegetables.

The layers comprised:

1. Canopy layer consisting of the original mature fruit trees
2. Low-tree layer of smaller nut and fruit trees on dwarfing rootstocks
3. Shrub layer of fruit bushes, such as currants and berries
4. Herbaceous layer of perennial vegetables and herbs
5. Rhizosphere, or underground, dimension of plants grown for their roots and tubers
6. Ground cover layer of edible plants that spread horizontally
7. Vertical layer of vines and climbers

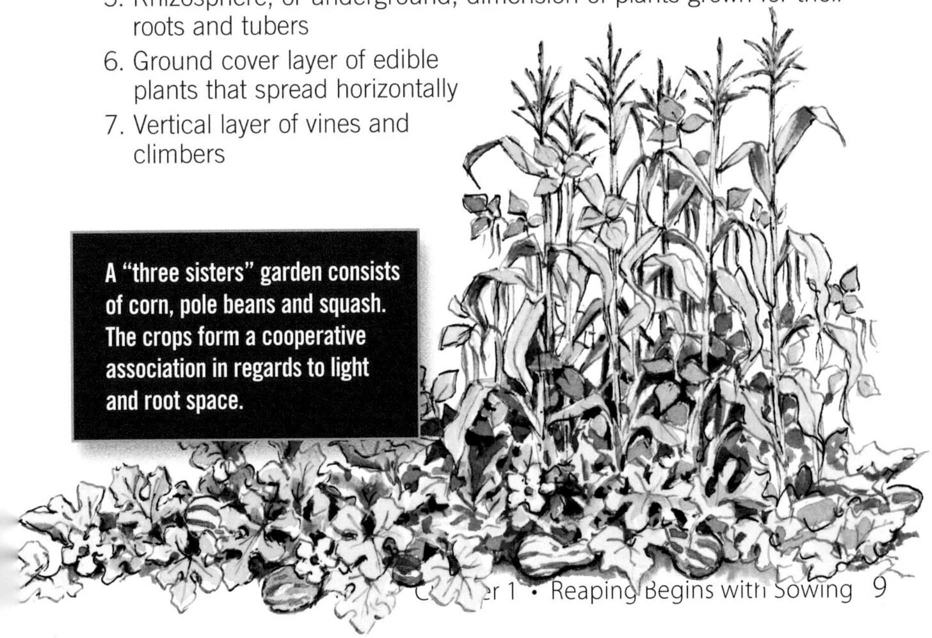

A "three sisters" garden consists of corn, pole beans and squash. The crops form a cooperative association in regards to light and root space.

leaves provide living mulch and shade for them all.

"Forest gardens" are probably the world's oldest form of agriculture and still one of the most resilient— and discreet. Since prehistoric times there has been a gradual process of identifying useful species and encouraging or planting them, and eliminating the undesirable or useless. Eventually, foreign species were selected and incorporated into the gardens, and gardens purpose-planted in disciplined shapes to accommodate efficient working and harvesting or, later, machines. In subsistence gardening, if you keep the original free form of forest gardens, scant use of machines is necessary. If you have a more or less permanent base, or at least a home area, but not your own woods, it can work to plant forage now and harvest later on land where you have access or acquiescence. When you come across a likely spot for a particular food plant, go for it. Just don't be like the squirrel frantically digging in the snow because he forgot where he put things Some of the basic tenets of "permaculture" are low maintenance and sustainability. With these come the additional benefits of low impact and low profile that translate for the purpose under discussion as less work and less risk of detection.

Heirloom Plants

Those willing to experiment have always enlarged the envelope of human experience. The net gain for our species isn't always worth the cost, some new developments ending up as a great leap ... but in the wrong direction. Such examples as uranium-based nuclear energy, genetically modified organism (GMO) plants, and socialism don't look like they will work out in the long run, and you can't help but notice that those who come up with these audaciously bright ideas usually like to let Mikey try it first whether or not he wants to.

So I'd reiterate the observation that nature likes to do what works in the long run, and in uncertain times of any kind it may be better to stick with what has proven itself to work. Audacity can win on the battlefield but not so much in the cornfield. When it comes to plants upon which your future meals may depend, a stick-in-the-mud mindset may be best. In other words, what you stick in the mud with hope it will feed you is probably better if it is an heirloom or heritage crop with a long history.

For market gardening or industrial agriculture, considerations necessarily include factors such as how handily a crop matures all at once for efficient harvest, how lovely it looks (not considering nutritional value), how well it adapts to shipping, and how long it can be stored before it spoils. For unattended or minimally nurtured survival gardening, however, different rules apply.

For our purposes here, I favor heirloom plants with a long track record

Paw Paw tree

Chapter 1

Acorns on oak tree

that makes them more predictable and literally more reproducible from seed. New hybrids produce seeds that, if even viable, may copy characteristics of their immediate parents or on back down their family tree and give results far from what you want. A prime example is the Cucurbitaceae family, which includes a hundred-plus genera, including *Curcubita* (e.g., squash, pumpkin, zucchini), *Lagenaria* (mostly inedible gourds), *Citrullus* (watermelons), and *Cucumis* (cucumbers)—and within this there are nearly a thousand species. Combined, they are among the oldest and most common plant families used as human food. Mostly annuals, although frost sensitive they grow from the tropics to temperate zones. With a little shelter, they thrive even in the Arctic, and with water they do well in desert climes.

So common are they that a vast array of hybrids has been developed, and most family garden plots will include members from several of these species. Thus, without protection to prevent cross-pollination, saved seed from a mixed plot is likely to produce a frankensquash result. I often let the next spring's volunteers mature just to see if I got lucky, but I very seldom do. The most common result has been hard, bitter, and gourd like.

I have no idea if they were a throwback to an original parent seed or a new and worthless hybrid. It would take more time and brains than I have to figure that out for sure, but for our purpose here it illustrates the benefit of truerunning heirloom seeds, which can include long-established hybrids, if you intend to harvest your own open-pollinated seeds for replanting.

The rationale for heirloom seeds transcends nostalgia or the fact that they are a tasty blast from the past. Varieties got to be heirloom because they have been selected over generations for taste and other positive aspects, not for their ease of shipping, uniform appearance, or ability to grow well throughout the entire area that seed catalogs fly. Ill-conceived laws now in place in Europe and proposed in the United States outlaw the sale of heirloom seeds that are not on "the list." A law proposed in Colombia actually outlawed an individual farmer's right to save his own seed for planting the next year. Published reports indicate that some 2,000 various cultivars have been lost in Europe alone, an ill result obviously beyond any condition that this wrong-headed regulation sought to correct. As the available gene pool shrinks, so does the ability to quickly develop new hybrids in response to new diseases or other changing conditions.

When gardeners save the seed of the best-tasting, best-performing plants for a number of years, they gradually develop their own special cultivars, which will be suited to their local growing conditions. Open-pollinated seeds that have been grown and harvested for generations in a region or microclimate become adapted to that area's soil, climate, and pests.

When politicians or apparatchiks propose to outlaw such a wholesome

activity, it makes one wonder if they are really that stupid or if they think the body politic is. As noted elsewhere, for a clandestine guerrilla garden, there is an advantage to planting perennials that feed you year after year, but this does not in any way negate the specific benefits that only some annuals, particularly vegetables, may bring. And when you plant those annuals, I think it is a good idea to plant heirlooms and save the seed. This is particularly true if you are growing seed for edible sprouts.

The nature-copying juxtaposition of plants practiced by Robert Hart does seem to work out in nature. Some planted as monoculture woods do survive to harvest as a single crop, such as a conventional tree farm, and some species do tend to eventually create a monoculture in certain areas where one species is particularly well served. But I've walked a lot of woods, and it has been observable overall that, barring any unique circumstances, most natural plots thrive when diverse, even as they evolve through the natural sequence that starts with annual plants, through brush, through deciduous trees, to predominantly evergreen forests. I'd hazard a guess that any stage of a forest's evolution would be suitable for adapting to a "forest" garden whether it is temperate-zone woods, sparse arid high country, or triple-canopy jungle. The individual plants, and the land, have a tremendous ability to adapt to what nature provides. This adaptability is key to their overall survival—and for the survival of our own species as well.

Man has more easily thrived in temperate-zone situations but has adapted well to the harsher choices of the Arctic and desert. The ability to adapt to hard climes and hard times is a skill set, or maybe an attitude, that is the linchpin not only of survival gardening but also survival per se. Attempting to force nature to adapt to us, or to always clean up our messes, just may be the ultimate folly. I would expect that nature will survive with us or without us. It's our call whether we want to tag along or fall off the edge kicking and screaming.

European wild garlic is invasive in North America, is similar to wild ramps, and is delicious.

The Oldest Heirlooms: Native Plants

Considering the wild origin of every domesticated plant species, uncounted wild plants in their native state still can be premium groceries. They worked for thousands of years to feed the hunter-gatherers who came before us. Many are still foraged in their natural state for the modern market: everything from purslane to wild onions to mushrooms to wild nuts/acorns to wild rice and various berries and so on are now readily found in American specialty markets, and the farther you get from the concrete jungle toward the triplecanopy jungle, the more common is produce that is harvested directly from the wild. And why not? Why mess with a system that works?

Cultivars that have been developed from wild plants may be barely recognizable from their ancestors, and the reverse is also true. The advantage to our discussion here is that the original plants may not look like food to a marauder and that native plants may be more readily suited to plant-and-neglect techniques. One advantage of purposeful agriculture has always been to increase the odds that a viable seed will end up as a useful mature plant. Thus if you take the time to sow and establish wild, native, edible plants, you can have harvestable crops from the wild, widely dispersed and largely unrecognizable to competing humans, and vastly increase the odds that competing animals will leave enough for you.

One technique to hide the fact that a technique has even been used is careful selection of companion plants that may tend to discourage your wild competitors. For instance, if you are considering establishing a "wild" bed of something that you anticipate ruminants to molest, plant in juxtaposition with wild onions or anything of the allium family, which many rodents find off-putting. Another technique that may fit your situation is to establish native species—such as purslane, Jerusalem artichokes, blackberries, or amaranth (a.k.a. red root pigweed)—that, once established, tend to compete very well and take over, yet to the unknowing are no more than weeds.

Depending on your location, there will be native, wild, edible plants that have never been a market item for commercial reasons and are often regarded as weeds, but which have fed local foragers since prehistoric times. Think local, plant local, and harvest local, wild, edible plants and you increase your odds for food growing without detection. Foraging the wild per se is a topic for another campfire, but encouraging or planting native forage crops is a facet of forest gardens to keep in mind, especially if you anticipate moving and revisiting specific areas. For an overview of edible forage plants common to temperate zones, I refer the reader to my earlier book *Eating on the Run*, a companion volume in this survival series from Ogden Publications.

Chapter 1

Amaranthus retroflexus

For your Daily Bread

Very little grain is produced today except in large fields. Grain crops are far more efficiently produced in a large block and seldom easy to produce in small stands. The following grains or cereals are probably the best adapted for isolated plants or haphazard weed patches that, if noticed, will probably be thought of as feral or bird-seeded.

• **Amaranth** A pseudo-cereal, amaranth (Amaranthus) was a staple in Mesoamerica before the Spaniards came and is enjoying a resurgence. Ancient amaranth grains still used to this day include the three species, *Amaranthus caudatus*, *Amaranthus cruentus*, and *Amaranthus hypochondriacus* (seen in the photo above).

The amaranth seed has much more protein than rice, and it is easy to harvest and cook. However, like the dandelion, it is so prolific that it is very invasive and a pest among other crops. Various strains have developed resistance to Roundup and other herbicides, and are enemy number one in soybean and cotton fields. Amaranth adapts very well to small plots. Plant it along a river bottom, and you get a crop, feed the birds, and irritate ConAgra all at the same time. The tender leaves are a good green, as well. Only cognoscenti will ever rob you of your amaranth, and if you see someone harvesting what you have sown, you may have met an ally. Seed heads can grow quite large and are an easy harvest if you beat the birds to them. In Mexico it is traditionally mixed with honey for a treat. It will grow well as a single plant among the other weeds. It will take what it gets as far as soil is concerned, but plant this in an old manure pile and stand back.

• **Corn** Heirloom varieties of dwarf corn would be my suggestion, as corn *(Zea mays)* that looks like corn, and a lot of it together, may draw attention. One prime advantage of corn is that you get a tremendous return on one seed, and the dried seed keeps very well for seed or food.

• **Milo** For many centuries, milo, or grain sorghum, has been one of the most important staples for millions of poor rural people in the hot, semi-arid areas of Asia and Africa, and is a principal source of energy, protein, vitamins, and minerals. Sorghum grows in harsh environments where other crops do not grow well. It is usually grown without fertilizers by small or subsistence farmers. Grain sorghum is the third-most-important cereal crop grown in the United States and the fifth-most-important cereal crop grown in the world. Sorghum molasses used to be popular down South, but most sorghum grown in the United States today goes for animal feed or export. It is of interest to us in a survival context because it is hardy and undemanding, and grows well as solitary plants or small stands.

• Wild Rice American Indians harvested wild rice (*Zizania palustris*) by tapping the ripe grains into a canoe with a stick, threshing the grain as it was harvested. Wild rice prefers constant water but grows in many drainage ditches in the northern Midwest, generally going to waste except for bird feed. Because of its good nutrition and taste, wild rice is commercially grown in the United States, Canada, Hungary, and Australia, and is harvested wild as a cash crop by Native Americans. Contrary to earlier belief, it will grow in still water, such as paddy fields for common (true) rice. Most of the U.S. crop is grown in California and Minnesota, but it can be found growing wild from the upper Midwest up into Canada. It is easily harvested by hand and easily cooked by boiling.

Good Neighbor Plants

MANY PLANTS SHOW A SYNERGISM when there are specific other plants in juxtaposition. Some just seem to grow well together, some offer protection against mutual enemies, some provide additional nutrition or condition the soil, and some, like mustard plants, act as sacrificial scapegoats to attract (trap) pests that would otherwise attack the crop you want to protect.

Here's a rundown on veggies that can help out in a wild garden with the mutual support some plants give to each other. This offering is not all-inclusive, and I have not personally tried every one of them, but the ones I have tried over the years did work well. Note that most of those listed here are annuals. There are certain no-care benefits to perennials, but more thought should be given to perennial selection, particularly if you want to plant annual crops among friendly perennials. Experiment locally. The compilation below is just an indication of the possibilities. I have seen it suggested that one should plant decoy food crops for human marauders, but this is not an idea I favor. Human marauders are seldom sated, and providing free samples is more likely to act as an attractant than anything. This, of course, is not to denigrate the idea of growing enough that one can selectively share his bounty, such as with the deserving needy. Of course, definitions of "deserving" vary. In his letter to the Thessalonians, Saint Paul noted, "If anyone is not willing to work, let him not eat." In case you dismiss the authority of scripture, Lenin agreed: "He who does not work shall not eat." Now, don't make me quote the Little Red Hen as well.

A common observation is that nature hates a vacuum, and you can see this illustrated in a fertile woods. If there is soil, water, and light, every spot has something growing in or under it, all jumbled together in a natural competition where every surviving plant got what it needed. Keep this in mind when you copy the style of nature in selecting what plants you will establish and how you will position them with other plants that will encourage or protect them. A meandering game trail is as close as nature gets to naked land between plants except after a fire in wild temperate zones. For our purpose, we do not want to waste any space or expose any tilled soil in either meandering or straight lines.

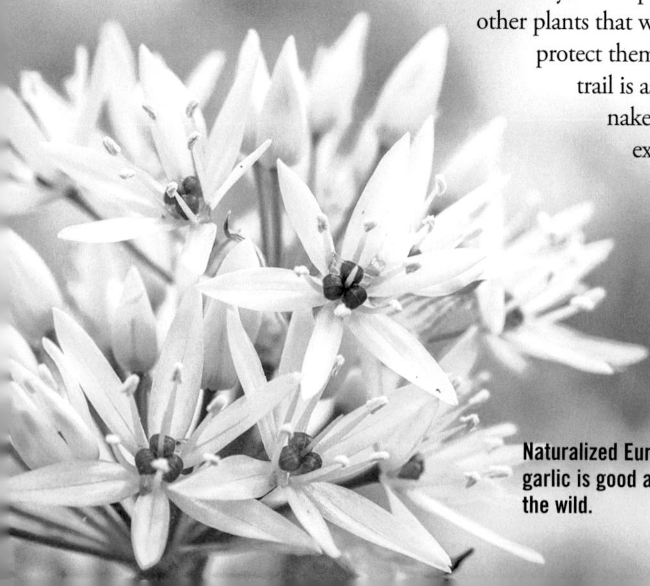

Naturalized European wild garlic flowers. All garlic is good and almost all will return to the wild.

Allium

• **Allium:** Allium is the genus of plants that includes onions, garlic, leeks, shallots, and chives. These plants help fruit trees, nightshades (e.g., tomatoes, capsicum peppers, potatoes), brassicas, and carrots, and in turn are helped by carrots, tomatoes, carrots, marigolds, and mints. Alliums attract thrips but repel or distract rabbits, slugs (see garlic), aphids, carrot fly, cabbage loopers, cabbage maggots, cabbage worms, and Japanese beetles. They don't get along so well with beans, peas, and parsley. A classic intercrop even in commercial gardens is a pairing of onions and carrots, examples of two veggies that just do well together. In a survival garden, you would place the plants more closely, in a random pattern, and possibly fill in between plants with something suitable, such as purslane.

• **Asparagus:** Asparagus *(Asparagus officinalis)*, a perennial, helps tomatoes and parsley, and itself is encouraged by aster family flowers, dill, coriander, tomatoes, parsley, basil, comfrey, marigolds, and nasturtiums. Working with basil, asparagus seems to encourage ladybugs. It doesn't get on well with onion, garlic, and potatoes.

Asparagus

Beans and Legumes

Beets

• **Beans and Legumes:** Beans and legumes *(Phaseolus* and *Vicia)* host nitrogen-fixing bacteria and thus are a good fertilizer for nitrogen-loving plants. Rosemary and peppermint extracts are used in organic sprays for beans. Summer savory and potatoes repel bean beetles. Beans and legumes help beets, lettuce, okra, potato, spinach, cabbage, carrots, chard, eggplant, peas, tomatoes, brassicas, corn, cucumbers, and grapes and in turn are helped by summer savory, beets, cucumbers, borage, cabbage, carrots, cauliflower, corn, larkspur, lovage, mustards, radish, potato, peppermint, rosemary, lettuce, onion, and squash. They attract snails and slugs, and repel Colorado potato beetle. They do not get on well with some alliums, tomatoes, or peppers.

• **Bush Beans:** Bush beans (*Phaseolus vulgaris*) are generally credited with being a good neighbor for cucumber and strawberries, and are welcomed by celery and grains. However, they are a contentious neighbor for fennel, soybeans, dry beans (according to some sources), and alfalfa. Various published sources say that lettuce, potato, tomato, other legumes, crucifers, or cucurbits increase Sclerotinia fungal pathogens in the soil and should be avoided before and after planting bush (snap) beans, and draw distinctions between green beans that sometimes imply a difference beyond the habit of pole or bush beans. My 50-year experience of picking bush beans for pay as a kid or growing them to eat as an adult has been that the difference between a green bean and a seed bean—except for kidney beans, red/black beans, pintos, limas, and the like—is a matter of how mature they are. My favorite garden bean is an heirloom from Eastern Europe the Czechs call a "magic bean." It is a bush bean that makes an excellent stringless green bean or, if left to mature, an excellent white "navy bean," and the seeds keep for many years. I don't know what to make of the assertion that green bean plants and seed bean plants never get along, unless they mean the ones just listed here, because in my case they usually are the same cultivar, sometimes different ends of the same plant. But the point here is, if you plant some here and some there, and next to plants they like, they usually do well and the nitrogen contribution from the organisms their roots harbor, in my experience, is not likely to cause a fungal outbreak.

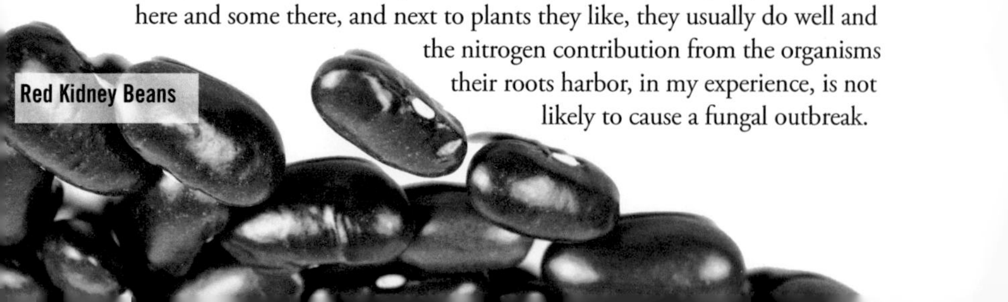

Red Kidney Beans

• **Beets:** Beets *(Beta vulgaris)* encourage broccoli, bush beans, cabbage, lettuce, kohlrabi, onions, brassicas, and like neighbors such as bush beans, onions (don't plant next to beans), kohlrabi, catnip, garlic, lettuce, most brassicas, and mint. Beets reportedly do not like runner or pole beans, which I think means the ones you eat as seed beans. Beet tops are great for compost and add a lot of minerals, but this is not a net gain unless you grew them somewhere else. I eat beet greens in preference to most other leafy veggies, anyway.

• **Brassicas:** Brassica is the genus that includes broccoli, Brussels sprouts, cabbage, cauliflower, Chinese cabbage, kohlrabi, radish, and turnip. Brassica plants have a good effect on plantings of beets, onions, potatoes, and cereal grains (e.g., corn, wheat), and show benefit from neighboring beets, spinach, chard, aromatic plants, or plants with many blossoms, such as celery, chamomile, marigolds, dill, sage, peas, peppermint, spearmint, spurrey, rosemary, rye grass, garlic, onions, potatoes, geraniums, alliums, nasturtiums, borage, hyssop, tansy, tomatoes, thyme, wormwood, southernwood, beans, and clover. They do not do as well next to mustards, nightshades (e.g., tomatoes, peppers), pole beans, or strawberries. They repel wireworms, and their own pests of cabbage worms, weevils, and cabbage loopers are discouraged by thyme, nasturtiums, and onion.

• **Carrots:** Carrots *(Daucus carota)* work well with tomatoes, alliums (e.g., chives, leeks, onions, shallots), beans, leeks, lettuce, and onions. They encourage lettuce, alliums, rosemary, wormwood, sage, and beans. Carrots attract the assassin bug, lacewing, parasitic wasp, yellow jacket, and other predatory wasps, while repelling the leek moth and onion fly thrips. They are not happy next to dill, parsnip, or radish. Tomatoes grow better with carrots but may stunt the carrots' growth. Beans provide the nitrogen that carrots need more than some vegetables. Aromatic companion plants repel carrot fly. Sage, rosemary, and radishes are recommended by some as companion plants but listed by others as incompatible. Alliums interplanted with carrots confuse onion and carrot flies. For the beneficial insect-attracting properties of carrots to work, they need to be allowed to flower (second year); alternatively, use wild carrot (Queen Anne's lace) for the same effect.

· **Celery:** Celery *(Apium graveolens)* helps bush beans, brassicas, and cucumbers, and loves cosmos, daisies, snapdragons, leeks, tomatoes, cauliflower, cabbage, and bush beans. Celery does not like corn.

• **Corn:** As noted in the last chapter, corn's scientific name is *Zea mays*. Beans, cucurbits, soybeans, and tomatoes like it as a neighbor, and in turn it is helped by sunflowers, dill, legumes (e.g., beans, peas, soybeans), peanuts, cucurbits, clover, amaranth, white geranium, pigweed, lamb's quarters, parsley, potato, field mustard, and Sudan grass. Corn does not like tomatoes or celery, and provides beans with a trellis. It is protected from predators and dryness by cucurbits, in the "three sisters" method of planting corn, beans, and squash together. Tall corn stalks can scream "garden" in a wild setting, but dwarf varieties are discreet yet still productive. Planting corn as a crop to encourage game animals is not unusual, so corn stalks are not always out of place in every sylvan setting!

• **Cucumbers:** Cucumbers *(Cucumis sativus)* help beans, kohlrabi, and lettuce, and in turn are helped by kohlrabi, nasturtiums, radishes, marigolds, sunflowers, peas, beans, chamomile, beets, carrots, dill, onions, garlic, amaranth, and celery. Cucumbers do not like spuds or aromatic plants. Sow two or three radish seeds in with cucumbers to repel cucumber beetles. One study showed a 75-percent reduction in cucumber beetles with the concurrent seeding of amaranth. If you plant amaranth seed and it comes up looking like redroot pigweed, well, that's what it commonly is, although there are many varieties. The various homemade sprays made from lettuce, asparagus, Malabar spinach, and celery have been found to reduce whiteflies.

- **Lettuce:** Lettuce *(Lactuca sativa)* helps beets, beans, okra, onions, radish, broccoli, Chinese cabbage, and carrots, and is encouraged by beets, beans, okra, onions, radish, broccoli, Chinese cabbage, and carrots. Lettuce attracts slugs and snails, and has antipathy for celery, cabbage, cress, and parsley. Mints (including hyssop, sage, and various balms) repel slugs common to lettuce and cabbages. Interestingly, when intercropped with lettuce, broccoli was shown to be more profitable than either crop alone.

- **Nightshades:** The nightshade *(Solanaceae)* family includes tomatoes, tobacco, chili peppers (including bell peppers), potatoes, eggplant, and others. In general nightshade plants help, and are helped by, carrots, alliums, and mints. Many are discouraged by beans, black walnuts, corn, fennel, dill, and brassicas.

- **Parsnips:** The flowers of the biennial parsnip *(Pastinaca sativa)* plant left to seed will attract a variety of predatory insects to the garden and are particularly helpful when left under fruit trees, with the predators attacking the codling moth and light brown apple moth. They thus are beneficial to a variety of fruit trees by attracting many predatory insects, and the root also contains myristricin, which is toxic to insects and mites.

Sugar Snap Peas

• **Peas:** Peas *(Pisum sativum)* help brassicas, turnips, cauliflower, and garlic, and are helped by turnips, cauliflower, garlic, and mint. Peas repel the Colorado potato beetle. It is of interest to preppers because it is a very early crop.

• **Peppers:** Peppers *(Solanaceae, Capsicum)* help okra and like the company of beans, tomatoes, marjoram, okra, geraniums, petunias, sunflowers, onions, crimson clover, basil, and field mustard. They don't like beans or cabbage family members such as kale, cabbage, and Brussels sprouts. Pepper plants like high humidity, which can be helped by planting with some kind of dense-leaf or ground-cover companion, like marjoram and basil; they also need direct sunlight, but their fruit can sunburn. Pepper plants grown together or with tomatoes can shelter the fruit from sunlight and raise the humidity level. Sunflowers, when in bloom at the right time, can shelter beneficial insects and lower thrip populations.

Peppers

• **Potatoes:** The potato plant *(Solanum tuberosum)* helps brassicas, beans, corn, and peas, and is encouraged by horseradish, beans, dead nettle, marigolds, peas, onion, garlic, thyme, and clover. The potato plant repels the Mexican bean beetle. Avoid planting it with carrots, cucumbers, pumpkins, squash, raspberries, sunflowers, and tomatoes. Horseradish increases the disease resistance of potatoes and repels the potato bug. Garlic spray was shown to be more effective than fungicides on late potato blight. Peas were shown to reduce the density of Colorado potato beetle populations.

• **Radish:** The radish *(Raphanus sativus)* is a good helper plant to squash, eggplant, cucumber, lettuce, peas, beans, and pole beans, and likes the company of chervil, lettuce, and nasturtiums. Don't plant radishes near grapes. They are a good trap crop for cucumber beetles and flea beetles.

• **Spinach:** Spinach *(Spinacia oleracea)* is beneficial to brassicas and cauliflower, and in turn benefits from nearby strawberries, peas, beans, and cauliflower. The peas and beans provide natural shade for the spinach. Cauliflower shows a mutualism with spinach.

• **Tomatoes:** The tomato *(Solanum lycopersicum)* is probably the most common of the nightshade family as a food, and is a boon to asparagus, broccoli, cabbage, celery, roses, and peppers. Tomatoes enjoy the company of basil, beans, bee balm (Monarda), oregano, parsley, marigold, alliums, celery, geraniums, petunias, nasturtium, borage, coriander, mustard, fenugreek, barley, carrots, eggplant, mints, okra, sage, and thyme. Tomatoes discourage the asparagus beetle. According to multiple sources, black walnuts inhibit tomato growth and are negatively allelopathic to all other nightshade plants as well because they produce a chemical called juglone. Dill attracts tomato hornworm. Tomatoes do not get on well with alfalfa, chili peppers (in a hothouse setting they increase tomato whitefly on the tomatoes), peas, potatoes, beets, brassicas, and rosemary. Some studies have shown that planting basil at 10-inch intervals with tomatoes can increase yield by up to 20 percent.

• **Turnips and Rutabagas:** Turnips *(Brassica rapa* and *Brassica napobrassica)* act as a trap crop for broccoli pests. Peas exhibit a mutualism with turnips. Turnips help peas and broccoli, and are helped by hairy vetch and peas. They don't like hedge mustard or knotweed.

Dandelion seeds

Some Weeds You Want

ACKNOWLEDGING THAT A WEED is just any plant that is growing where you do not want it to be, I will list these weeds separately from the other good neighbor companion plants. Some here are decent victuals in their own right, while some have scant use except as noted. But for our consideration here, they all have the advantage of being notorious weeds and, if used to your advantage in a clandestine food plot, help give the illusion of a weed patch as opposed to a garden.

- **Amaranth:** Generally called pigweed, amaranth is an excellent survival seed. The most common amaranth example in North America is red-root pigweed.

- **Bashful Mimosa:** Bashful mimosa *(Mimosa pudica)* acts as a host for predatory beetles and is used as a natural ground cover in agriculture. In contemporary medicine, it is being investigated for its potential to yield novel chemotherapeutic compounds. It contains an alkaloid called mimosine, which has been found to have potent antiproliferative and apoptotic effects on cancer cells.

- **Caper Spurge:** Caper spurge *(Euphorbia lathyris)* repels moles and is used in folk medicine as an antiseptic and purgative. Many domesticated animals can eat it, although it is poisonous to humans.

• **Clover:** Clover *(Trifolium)* distracts rabbits and helps such brassica crops as cabbage and cousins like broccoli and cauliflower, plus corn, cucurbits (e.g., cucumber, squash, melons, and gourds). Along with fertilizing the soil as a legume that hosts nitrogen-fixing bacteria in its roots, clover provides a humid microclimate that benefits many plants by stabilizing their moisture and therefore fertilizing the soil for neighboring plants. It is also used as a fallow plant and is a common fodder plant. It is a high-protein green and rich in vitamin C. It does not get along with nightshades.

• **Cocklebur:** Cocklebur *(Xanthium)* repels armyworms. Although poisonous to some livestock, it is used in Chinese medicine and as a yellow dye.

• **Crow Garlic:** Crow garlic *(Allium vineale)* gets along well with fruit trees, nightshades, brassicas, and carrots but does not play well with beans, peas, and parsley. It repels slugs, aphids, carrot fly, and cabbage worms. A wild cousin of onions and garlic, crow garlic can be used like conventional chives. The 3-mercapto-2-methylpentanol compound in onion was found to have an antioxidant property that inhibits peroxynitrite-induced diseases.

• **Dandelion:** Dandelion *(Taraxacum)* repels armyworms and attracts bees. Its taproot breaks up hardened soil and brings up nutrients from deep down, benefiting plants with weaker or shallower roots without competing with them. Its leaves and flowers are edible as a favorite spring potherb or tender leaves in salads. It is used as a diuretic in herbal medicine.

• **Goldenrod:** Goldenrod *(Solidago)* attracts predatory wasps, repels various Lepidoptera (moth) larva, and has many medicinal uses. It is also a viable source of latex (the automobile given to Thomas Edison by Henry Ford had tires made from goldenrod latex). Of course, avoid it or place carefully if you are allergic to it.

• **Ground Ivy:** Ground ivy *(Glechoma hederacea)* is a wild mint that gets along well with tomatoes, peppers, cucumbers and their relatives (squash, melons), broccoli, Brussels sprouts, and cauliflower. It repels cabbage worms, cucumber worms and beetles, tomato hornworms, and other pests. It makes a good ground cover companion plant, creating a humid microclimate, covering up nearby plant scents, and distracting pests from companion crops. Ground ivy can be used in herbal teas and has been used in traditional European medicine for thousands of years to treat inflammation of the eyes, tinnitus, and as a diuretic, astringent, tonic, and gentle stimulant.

• **Horse Nettle:** Horse nettle *(Solanum carolinense)* attracts predatory beetles. Herbalists use cooked ripe fruit as a diuretic and sedative.

• **Milkweed:** Milkweed *(Asclepias)* helps corn, basil, and potatoes; attracts predatory wasps and the Monarch butterfly; and repels wireworms. It is a traditional folk remedy for warts, and its sap reduces the discomfort of poison ivy/oak/sumac. Basil repels some insects that attack milkweed. Seed down can be used as a more effective insulator than goose down. Milkweed emits a chemical that breaks up hard soil, allowing adjacent plants to develop healthier root systems.

Nasturtium

• **Nasturtium:** Nasturtium *(Tropaeolum)* is pretty much a silver bullet companion plant, benefiting almost any crops around it in some way, and not known to hurt any. Most vegetables—especially brassicas, cucurbits, and solanum—like it. It attracts predatory wasps and repels squash bugs, cucumber beetles, striped pumpkin beetles, and woolly aphids, and acts as a sacrificial trap crop for caterpillars and black aphids. Further, all parts of this plant are edible, and its flowers and leaves make striking salad decorations. It is sometimes found as a feral wild plant, but so worthwhile that it's worth figuring some way to work it into your plot or flower box if nothing else.

• **Nettle:** Nettle *(Urtica dioica)* grows synergistically with broccoli, tomato, valerian, mint, and fennel. It is one of the most common plants in herbal medicine, with a long list of benefits. Its tender buds and leaves are tasty, and the plant is also grown as a crop for its fiber. Its sting repels all thin-skinned mammals.

• **Purslane:** Purslane *(Portulaca oleracea)* is a delicious companion to corn and solanums, such as tomatoes and peppers. It contains more omega-3 fatty acids than any other leafy vegetable plant. It can be eaten in salads, stir fried, or cooked like spinach. Berries can be eaten like capers. In traditional Chinese medicine, it is used to treat infections or bleeding of the genitourinary tract, as well as to combat dysentery. It may also be applied topically to relieve sores and insect or snake bites on the skin. Dill, parsnip, and radish don't like it, but it breaks up hard soil and hardpan, brings nutrients and water up from deeper than other crops can reach, provides healthy ground cover, and stabilizes soil moisture. It is one of my favorite weeds and recently has started appearing in yuppie restaurants.

• **Queen Anne's Lace:** Queen Anne's lace *(Daucus carota)*, or wild carrot, is a happy neighbor to nightshades (especially tomatoes), alliums, and lettuce. It does not like dill, radishes, or (surprisingly) parsnips. Its young roots are edible.

• **Wild Mustard:** All mustards *(Brassicaceae)* make good trap plants for various brassica pests, including aphids. Mustard plants benefit grape vines, radishes, and nonmustard brassicas—including cabbage, cauliflower, and broccoli—but not beets. Seeds and leaves are edible. Domesticated mustard is a hybrid of three different species of wild mustard.

• **Wild Rose:** Wild rose belongs in the Rosa genus. Various species, including the feral "multiflora rose" planted as a living hedge, have in many areas become invasive. It gets along well with strawberries, grapes, and roses; attracts rodents and deer; and traps Japanese beetles.

• **Wild Vetch:** Wild vetch *(Vicia americana)* encourages pepper and tomato plants, brassicas, and other plants needing high levels of nitrogen, as it is a legume that fixes nitrogen (let it grow in a tomato garden only until planting time, as ground cover). It can be left growing among brassicas for additional nitrogen and microclimate. It provides ground cover for predatory beetles.

Planting for Protection

PLANTING BARRIER PLANTS is an old practice. Agriculturists not wanting to share the fruits of their labor with outsiders or competing livestock have been surrounding their plots with thorny plants throughout recorded history. The technique can be readily but discreetly expanded to include plants that are offensive to creatures great and small, including plants that are toxic to animals and insects. In a plot that is untended or, if tended, is being raised without purchased products, insecticides, or repellents that you grow or produce yourself, planting barrier plants may be the only game in town.

Barrier plants

For general use, a barrier plant's effectiveness begins as a visible deterrent, but for our specific use, we do not want to make it look like we are protecting something. Cyclone fences and concertina wire make it obvious there is something of interest and worth protecting behind it, and so will non-native species of plants unless they are commonly used in the area and can be made to look like they are native or have merely gone wild.

Fortunately, most climes have a native or very common selection of plants that discourage intrusion without looking like they are there for that purpose. Use what is appropriate to your locale; plants can vary from unfriendly to hazardous.

Thoughtful planning is worth a lot because every site and its security requirements will be different. A common tack to take is to put "deterrent" plantings at your perimeter where they will deter but not necessarily harm casual non-invitees, and then place more serious barrier plants the closer they get to an exclusion zone. Plan so the barrier plants act as, but do not look like, a purposeful feature. Most of these plants that learned to fight back developed their harsh weapons for defense in harsh conditions, so overall they do not need much coddling to flourish.

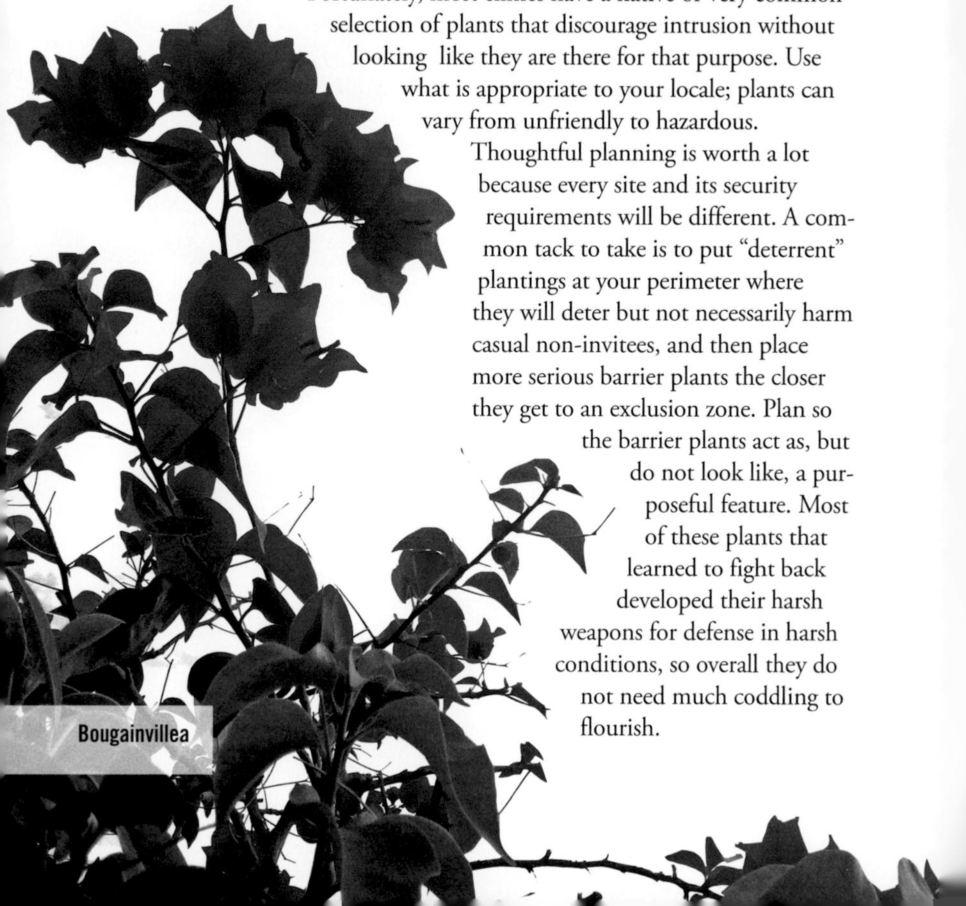

Bougainvillea

Perennials make the best barrier plants because they and their protection never wane, and woody varieties keep on growing until you cut them back, allowing you to train them to their most effective form for security purposes. Thus, planning starts with selecting the species best adapted to your climate. The good news is that there are appropriate species no matter where you are, and odds are that, as common local flora, they will not draw attention.

At an area perimeter, barriers comprising woody perennials can work synergistically with smaller plants, such as nettles or brambles. Decide which areas are vulnerable and then plan and plant accordingly, with an eye to keeping it all looking as happenstance. Remember, barrier plants never sleep, never make noise like a dog, and don't require feeding.

Here's a list of commonly used barrier plants from which you can pick ideas as to what would not be noticeable in your situation. In the desert southwest, you can take your pick of good native barrier plants, but the barrenness of the environs makes any human activity pretty obvious.

Teddy Bear Cholla

Sweet Aracia

• **Agave:** a.k.a. century plant. All varieties can be planted close for an impenetrable thicket; some grow quite large.

• **Barberry:** Many cultivars of this spiny-shrubby bush do well in colder climates. It is a popular security plant in the United Kingdom.

• **Barrel Cactus:** This plant has serious thorns and needs moderate space.

• **Blackberry:** Himalayan or other classic varieties are not thornless cultivars. "Innocent" and effective, just ask Bre'r Rabbit. This vine is not a perfect deterrent to deer or goats, as they browse the new growth, nor for pigs who dig up the roots. But dead inner vines are a deterrent to walk-through guests, although not to rodents who like a brier patch for the protection it provides.

Barrel Cactus

Blackberry

Devil's Club

Hawthorn

Hedgehog Cactus

Pomegranate

Agave

Prickly Pear

Honey Locust

Holly

Ocotillo

- **Blackthorn:** From Europe but available in the United States, it has serious long thorns and is a little invasive.

- **Bougainvillea:** Popular decorative vine worldwide, it is beautiful and very spiky.

- **Cholla, staghorn:** Branching varieties provide good harassing deterrent.

- **Cholla, teddy bear:** When you care enough to plant the very best: any man or beast that tangles with this will remember it. It is easy to plant and requires minimum maintenance. Note: Spines contain highly flammable oil; do not plant close to flammable structures.

- **Desert Acacia:** a.k.a. "sweet acacia," "cat-claw" or "wait-a- minute" bush.

- **Devil's Club:** This is a good deterrent for the woods of the western United States, and its large palmate leaves also make a good visual screen.

- **Hardy Orange:** a.k.a. bitter orange, trifoliate orange, and Japanese bitter orange; related to citrus family. King of the commercial barrier plants, hardy orange forms cruel and impenetrable thickets, but it is an attractive plant.

- **Hawthorn:** This plant makes a dense hedge 20-feet high with 1- to 5-inch thorns and pretty pink flowers. It can live to be hundreds of years old.

• **Hedgehog Cactus:** Strong boots can defeat this cactus, but it makes nice beds and borders.

• **Holly:** Holly has many cultivars, does well in colder climates, makes a small tree, prunes/shapes well, and is not uncommon as bird-seeded or feral plantings.

• **Locust:** Honey locust can be planted as a deterrent to men, animals, or vehicles. A strong and easily transplanted tree, it has world-class thorns.

• **Nettle:** a.k.a. common nettle or stinging nettle, it has many hollow, stinging hairs called trichomes on the leaves and stems, which act like hypodermic needles, injecting histamine and other chemicals that sting. The plant has long been used as food and medicine, and for its flax-like fiber. Native all over, nettles look at home anywhere.

• **Ocotillo:** a.k.a. coral bush. In its clime, it can be planted very close and dense. With its serious thorns, untrained it makes a large wand-like planting. It has pretty red flowers after a good rain.

• **Oregon Grape:** A brushy, low, native mimic of holly.

• **Osage Orange:** This American native is related to ebony. Millions have been planted for windbreaks and erosion control. It forms a strong, spiny, impenetrable hedge.

Yucca

• **Pomegranate:** Older varieties form a warm-climate thicket that looks "open" but is prickly and thick.

• **Prickly Pear:** Spineless hybrids are worthless except for food, but most states have a native species that is high on the discomfort list and has edible leaves and fruit.

• **Pyracantha:** Popular ornamental that trains like a vine up a wall or will make a good bush or hedge. It has attractive flowers, deep orange berries, and A-1 thorns!

• **Rose:** This plant is beyond criticism when it comes to providing protection in most jurisdictions. Select for strong stalks and large thorns. "Mermaid" is beautiful, sporting clear yellow blooms, whereas "Voodoo" has world-class thorns.

• **"Russian olive":** Neither an olive nor from Russia, this invasive tree is controlled in some jurisdictions. It can be trained into a strong, thorny thicket. It has edible drupes.

• **Saguaro Cactus:** Because of its serious thorns, you must have space between plants.

Chili Peppers
and Lavender

• **Siberian Pea Shrub:** This shrub/tree is cold- and drought-hardy, trains well, can be grown in movable pots, and sports pretty flowers and edible fruit.

• **Thorny Palm:** This low-growing tree has sawlike thorns on frond stems.

• **Yucca:** a.k.a. Spanish bayonet, the yucca has many varieties, some cold-hardy. All make good barriers.

Natural pest-repellent plants

Repellent plants are passive compared to barrier plants, but in many instances can work better. For instance, I don't know of any barrier plants that will exclude small rodents and insects, but an effective repellent plant can keep them out by making them not want to go there. Some of those listed on pages 54–62 are for a specific pest, and some for a class of pests; some are only good as a repellent, and some have additional culinary or medicinal uses. Some can be invasive, such as citronella grass, which is a perennial that is inedible to all grass eaters. Consider these aspects before you plant.

There are other repellent techniques besides passive plantings that create undesirable environs for a particular pest. Appropriate, pest-specific repellents can be dusted (e.g., pepper flakes/powders, human hair) or sprayed (e.g., homemade allium concoctions; human or canine urine can do double duty as both fertilizer and repellent). Hot pepper powders proved to be a quick temporary fix to stop browsers when I had it on hand. The adventure of growing, drying, and finely milling habaneros is a story for another undertaking. If peppers do not thrive in your area, dried mustard seed, dried horseradish root, or dried skunk cabbage root may provide an uncomfortable level of heat.

Various predator urine (e.g., bear for deer, wolf/coyote for rodents) can be effective, but don't expect your local outdoor shop to be operating in interesting times.

Some "repellents" also discourage effective predation from pests by confusing the pest, in effect camouflaging the crop with scents from other plants such as mints, alliums, marigolds, or chrysanthemum, and of these some will merely repel one creature (e.g., alliums vs. rodents) and yet poison another (e.g., mums vs. insects), while not affecting man.

I have seen witches' brews made of garlic, tobacco "tea," ground chrysanthemums, mint, liquid soap, and other ingredients that do seem to keep the bugs out of home gardens, but a man could smell them from the street, which is not a good idea for our purpose. I once read of a technique for discouraging an infestation of specific insects that was to catch/trap a quantity

Artemisia

Basil

Borage

Castor Bean

of the offending bug, grind them up, let them ferment a day or two, mix thinly with unscented soap, and spray on affected crops. The theory was that species would recognize their own dead and not go where something was killing them. It seemed to work, but by the time I did all this they had mostly moved on anyway. I prefer to compost dead things before putting them on a food crop and use repellent plants, which so far have seemed to be most effective and, by far, the most labor effective. But if you happen to have handpicked or trapped a particular critter, this is something you might want to try. See further on for recipes for home-brew bug-getters, most of which can be made from homegrown plant ingredients.

Remember the NCO biting at your heels not to bunch up on a route march? "Spread out, spread out ... one round will get you all," he'd scream. And he was right. The Roman phalanx worked OK for maintaining control of a force in the days when they were still throwing rocks and arrows at each other, but in modern war a concentrated gaggle of troops is what the enemy calls a "target-rich environment." It's the same in a garden: Normally working as browsers, marauding ruminants, rodents, and bugs love to find a tidy row of their favorite lunch, handily prepared for them like the vegetable section in a market. Before sunup they will have marched down a row of prime produce like Sherman through Georgia.

Pick plants that like each other, pick repellent plants that work with them, and plant in a disorganized fashion that forces a marauder to search for his dinner among plants he doesn't care for, that he finds offensive, or that confuse him with their scent. This not only confuses critters, it also helps mask a garden from two-legged grocery-grabbers as well. Check out the companion plants in Chapter 2.

Plants that can be planted or used fresh to deter pests include, but are not limited to, those listed below. Note that there are crossover benefits, such as all alliums or all mints, although a specific repellent ability is noted. They may be used in companion planting for pest control in garden situations or inside.

- **Artemisia:** Various types of sage repel insects, including ants, cabbage looper, cabbage maggot, carrot fly, codling moth, flea beetles, whiteflies, cabbage white "moths," and the small white butterfly, as well as mice.

- **Basil:** Repels flies, including mosquitoes and the carrot fly, plus asparagus beetles and whiteflies.

- **Borage:** Repels tomato hornworm and cabbage worms by confusing the egg-layers; borage is touted as a good companion plant to tomatoes.

- **Castor Bean:** Repels moles; its seeds and extracts are deadly poisonous to mammals.

- **Catnip:** Repels ants, flea beetles, aphids, the Japanese beetle, squash bugs, weevils, the Colorado potato beetle, the cabbage looper, and cockroaches.

Catnip

Chamomile

Chives

Chrysanthemum

Citronella Grass

Clover

Common
Lantana

Crown
Imperial

Coriander

Dahlia

Cosmos

Dill

Eucalyptus

Fennel

Four o'Clocks

French Marigold

- **Chamomile:** Repels flying insects and makes a fine relaxing tea.
- **Chives:** Repel carrot fly, Japanese beetle, and aphids.
- **Chrysanthemum:** Repels roaches, ants, Japanese beetle, ticks, silverfish, lice, fleas, bedbugs, and root-knot nematodes. The plant contains pyrethrins that are deadly to most insects.
- **Citronella Grass:** Repels most insects and deters some cats. Do not confuse with edible lemongrass from Southeast Asia.
- **Clover:** Repels aphids and wireworms.
- **Common Lantana:** Repels mosquitoes. This naturalized, invasive shrub was originally an ornamental; it likes warmer climates.
- **Coriander:** (Cilantro) repels aphids, the Colorado potato beetle, and spider mites.
- **Cosmos:** Repels the corn earworm, adapts well, and volunteers year after year in most gardens.
- **Crown Imperial:** Repels rabbits, mice, moles, voles, and ground squirrels. It is a lily that smells like a fox.
- **Dahlia:** Repels nematodes.
- **Dill:** Repels aphids, squash bugs, spider mites, cabbage looper, tomato hornworm, and the small white butterfly. It is called "dill weed" for good reason—it is easy to grow but hardy and seeds heavily and can take over.
- **Eucalyptus:** a.k.a. "silver dollar plant" repels aphids, cabbage looper, and Colorado potato beetle.
- **Fennel:** Repels aphids, slugs, and snails.

Garlic

Larkspur

Geranium

Lavender

Hyssops

Leek

Lemon Thyme

Lettuce

Lime Basil

Mexican Marigold

- **Four o' Clocks:** Attracts and poisons Japanese beetles. It is mostly grown as an ornamental.

- **French Marigold:** This genus, Tagetes, repels whiteflies and kills nematodes (see Mexican Marigold, page 61). Often planted commercially with tomatos, eggplants, chili peppers, tobacco, and potatoes. Due to antibacterial thiophenes exuded by the roots, these should not be planted near any legume crop, as it has a bad effect on the nitrogen-fixing bacteria hosted by the legume roots. Some perennial species are deer, rabbit, rodent, and javelina resistant.

- **Garlic:** Repels aphids, Japanese beetle, carrot fly, codling moth, snails, root maggots, cabbage looper, Mexican bean beetle, peach tree borer, small rodents, and rabbits. Finely ground garlic in a water solution and used as a spray is not just a repellent, it also kills many insects and larvae.

- **Geranium:** Repels leafhoppers, corn earworm, and small white butterfly. (Most window box and houseplant "geraniums" are actually Pelargoniums, a related species that serves our same purpose here.)

- **Hyssop:** Repels the cabbage looper and small white butterfly.

- **Larkspur:** Repels aphids.

- **Lavender:** Repels moths, fleas, and flies, including mosquitoes. Dried, it makes a good moth-repellent indoors.

- **Leek:** Repels the carrot fly.

- **Lemon Balm:** Repels mosquitoes. In the mint family, lemon balm can be used as a flavoring.

Narcissus

Oregano

Nasturtium

Parsley

Onion

Radish

Spearmint

Petunia

Sage

- **Lemon Thyme:** Repels mosquitoes. A perennial shrub, lemon thyme is used as a flavoring.
- **Lettuce:** Repels carrot flies and can be a trap crop for slugs.
- **Lime Basil:** Repels mosquitoes.
- **Mexican Marigold:** Repels insects and rabbits and is a specific repellent for flea beetles. Plant grows quickly, providing protection a few days after sprouting (see French Marigold).
- **Narcissus:** Repels moles, rodents, and, by some accounts, deer when planted at the drip line of trees. Yes, a daffodil is a narcissus.
- **Nasturtium:** Repels whiteflies, squash bugs, aphids, many beetles, and cabbage loopers. The entire plant is edible as well.
- **Onion:** Repels rabbits, cabbage loopers, and the small white butterfly. (See also Garlic, Leeks.)
- **Oregano:** Repellent to many insects and small mammals.
- **Parsley:** Repels asparagus beetles. Peppermint. Repels aphids, cabbage loopers, flea beetles, squash bugs, whiteflies, and the small white butterfly, as well as geese and rodents. (See also Spearmint, page 62.)
- **Petunia:** Repels aphids, tomato hornworms, asparagus beetles, leafhoppers, and squash bugs.
- **Radish:** Repels cabbage maggots and cucumber beetles (plant a few with cucumbers).

Rosemary

Common Rue

Tansy

Tobacco

- **Rosemary:** Repels cabbage loopers, carrot flies, slugs, snails, and the Mexican bean beetle, as well as such ruminants as deer, rodents, and rabbits.

- **Rue:** Repels cucumber and flea beetles. It can cause skin blisters. It is used, but not recommended, as a seasoning.

- **Sage:** Friendly to bees but not sucking and crawling bugs.

- **Spearmint:** Repels fleas, moths, ants, beetles, rodents, aphids, squash bugs, and cabbage loopers. (See also Peppermint.)

- **Spiny Amaranth:** Repels cutworms. It readily goes native and has edible seeds and edible young leaves.

- **Summer Savory:** Repels bean beetles. It is a popular sage-type seasoning native to North America.

- **Tansy:** Repels ants, many beetles and flies, squash bugs, cutworms, the small white butterfly, and the cabbage white "moth." Many people are allergic to its pollen. It is a legally controlled pest in some areas as it can take over, killing other plants and creating a fire hazard.

- **Thyme:** Repels cabbage loopers, cabbage maggots, corn earworms, whiteflies, tomato hornworms, and small white butterflies.

- **Tobacco:** Repels carrot flies and flea beetles. Its leaves can be leached for use as an insecticide spray.

- **Tomato:** Repels asparagus beetles.

Go Proactive:

Less-Than-Lethal

Killers

Chrysanthemum

HERE, OF COURSE, I MEAN PRETTY SAFE FOR HUMANS but unhealthy or deadly for marauding wildlife. In addition to just planting specimens that bugs avoid because they are toxic, you can make extracts from these plants and other benign-to-human sources and use them as a weapon against pests.

Natural pesticides: homgrown, low-impact

In this context, "home-grown" is used in a literal sense. Most of the plants mentioned here are ones you can grow for this purpose or you may already have them around your place. Most of the repellent plants in the previous chapter work for our purpose by simply turning bugs away due to their aroma or other properties. That's fine by me since they'll still make a lunch for some beneficial predatory bug or bird and stay out of my work. However, some plants, such as the chrysanthemum, are deadly to most insects due to their pyrethrin content. Except for individuals with a rare allergy to mums, they usually have no effect on man; chrysanthemum tea is common in China and regarded as therapeutic. So effective and otherwise benign are pyrethrins that they have been widely synthesized for agricultural and consumer use. My own observation over the years has been that marauding bugs either go for the best and brightest plants, like man, or attack the weaker specimens, like a natural wolf pack stalking a winter herd. This gardener's response has been to try to maintain healthy plants so they can fight off, or survive, bug predation. Or maybe with a little luck, look strong and unappealing, if my theory of target selection by bugs is correct. Sickly plants are often associated with pest infestations. It's irrelevant to me which is cause and which is effect.

The use of bug killers goes hand in hand with the use of repellent and sacrificial plants as mentioned earlier. In general, it's good to react to bugs quickly, especially in a hothouse or other finite-environment setting. The life cycle of many pests is so accelerated that some can reproduce and thrive in no time if left untreated. If you have the time and inclination to hand-pick such things as potato beetles or tomato hornworms, the best time to do so is when they are cold and slow moving, usually early in the morning. The best time to apply various home-brewed concoctions is on a cool, dry afternoon. Natural toxins almost universally have the ability to break down in the soil by themselves, as opposed to the chlorinated hydrocarbons and toxic metal salts of which modern chemists have grown so fond.

• **Rhubarb leaf mix:** Rhubarb contains oxalic acid, which gives the stalks their tartness, but the leaves have toxic quantities. To make a spray for aphids, June bugs, spider mites, and thrips, finely mince about a pound of rhubarb leaves, cover with about a half-gallon of water in a heat-safe glass bowl, and bring to a boil and cook for half an hour. Set aside until cool and then strain. Add a couple tablespoons of liquid dish soap, stir, and spray as needed. Be careful around corroded metal, as the concoction will dissolve oxidized metal, such as copper or zinc, which may then contaminate the soil. After harvesting rhubarb for pies, instead of just adding the leaves to the compost, I usually use them for mulch.

• **Rotenone:** Rotenone is extracted from seeds and stems of certain plants, specifically the ones common to North America listed below. It is deadly to insects and fish and, though thought to be only mildly toxic to humans, has been associated with incidence of Parkinson's disease in exposed farm-workers. It particularly kills potato beetles, cucumber beetles, flea beetles, cabbage worms, raspberry beetles, and asparagus beetles, as well as most other arthropods. It rapidly biodegrades under warm conditions, so harmful residues are minimal. A light dusting on the leaves of plants will control insects for several days. In many cases, as with flea beetles, I have found they may be an infestation that was apparently just traveling through, and I often do not have to reapply agents.

Hoary Pea

Jicama

• **Hoary Pea** *(Tephrosia virginiana)*: Also known as goat's rue, hoary pea is native to areas in the midwest to eastern United States. Stems were once crushed and used as a fish killer. All parts of the plant are toxic to man and domestic animals. Using careful hygiene, mill the plant, dry, and scatter in the area you want to protect, avoiding water courses.

• **Jicama** *(Pachyrhizus erosus):* Commonly cultivated in Mexico and similar North American climes for its delicious root, jicama seeds contain a high proportion of rotenone, as do the stems. The seeds are dried, milled, and used as a dust.

• **Florida Fishpoison Tree** *(Piscidia piscipula)*: Natives of southern Florida and the Caribbean have traditionally used its bark extract to stun fish, as it contains rotenone and sedative compounds. The bark extract is leached, filtered, and sprayed for bug control.

• **Oleander:** Oleander is such a common shrub worldwide that it has never been determined exactly from whence it came, although most think it originally came from Southeast Asia. It is also famously poisonous and, from this, over the last couple centuries at least, urban legends have abounded. The current yarn, of some Boy Scouts who roasted hot dogs on oleander sticks and died, originally appeared some 200 years ago. Another tale is of some marauding French soldiers in Spain, of which seven of twelve died after using oleander as skewers for stolen meat. Not. Horses and cattle are particularly susceptible to its poisonous effects, but it would take about 100 grams (about 3 ounces) to kill a horse. I have witnessed this happen when horses ate oleander trimmings, but as a viable do-it-yourself pest control agent, it is essentially worthless. However, there is record of it being used successfully as an agent for suicide, and accidental poisonings have sickened many over the years. It is not worth the effort for pest control.

- **Castor Oil Plant:** Another famously poisonous plant is the castor oil plant, from which ricin (a strong poison) and undecylenic acid (an old standby treatment for fungus, in particular ringworm and athlete's foot) are extracted. More than a million tons a year of castor "beans" (the seed) are produced, primarily for the castor oil, which is used as a lubricant, emollient, laxative, or in candy as a substitute for cocoa butter. It is a widely used ornamental plant in freeze-free zones, even growing wild in some city parks in Los Angeles. The plant's ricin content is sufficient to provide some protection against such insect pests as aphids. Ricin poisoning occurs when animals, including humans, ingest broken seeds or break the seed by chewing: intact seeds may simply pass through. Toxicity varies among target species: four seeds will kill a rabbit, five a sheep, six a cow or horse, seven a pig, and eleven a dog. In tests it took an average of 80 to kill a duck, but I suspect ducks may have a total immunity and died from a ruptured crop. Pure ricin is difficult to extract, but it has been weaponized, and during the Cold War was used in some high-profile assassinations. A dose of purified ricin equivalent to a few grains of table salt can kill an adult human. As a pest-control device, three or four of the attractive seeds are soaked overnight in water and placed inside a mole tunnel or gopher run. When I was a kid

Oleander

Castor Beans

Chili Peppers

in Oregon, where moles are one of a rural gardener's continual problems, ricin seed seemed to work almost as well as running a hose from the exhaust on a Model A Ford, pulling out the choke a little, and gassing them. The farm store would have open baskets of the castor seeds for sale cheap, with instructions to place them well down in a mole hole to keep them away from livestock. Moles primarily stockpile and eat worms, but they like nuts and castor beans.

• **Hot Peppers:** Run a cup or so of fresh hot peppers (depending on their Scoville rating) through a blender until well ground. Add to a quart of near-boiling water, throw in a jigger of vodka, mix well but gently, and let steep uncovered overnight for the alcohol, used as an extractive solvent, to evaporate. Then add a teaspoon of unscented dish detergent. Mix slowly, strain through a coffee filter, and administer with a hand sprayer. This concoction deters a variety of pests, but don't spray directly on crops you plan to eat. I once pepper-sprayed a raccoon eating the grapes on the arbor under my eaves and later had to discard the ones dyed red as they were too hot. In this recipe you can also substitute a couple of teaspoons of cayenne powder and dust it on or near plants; or you can dry and mill the peppers you have (especially the seeds) and do the same. I had an old woods-living buddy who had deer eating his beets and he dusted around them with this homemade powder. Worked fine: it made the deer sneeze, which woke up his past-retirement, pot-licking dog, who would then stagger off the porch and chase them away.

• **Citrus Spray:** Citrus oil has microbicidal and insecticidal properties, especially against small flyers such as white flies. Grind a couple of cups of citrus peel (e.g., orange, lemon, grapefruit). Bring a gallon of water to a boil and set aside. Add the ground citrus peel with a shot of vodka (or rubbing alcohol) and steep until cold. Strain and apply liberally with a mist-type hand sprayer; if spraying outside, wait for a calm day. Always test on a single plant before going whole hog.

• **Garlic Tea:** Most critters, from rodents to ruminants to crawling and flying insects, are offended by members of the allium family, such as garlic or onions. To some insects, the aromatic sulfur compounds that alliums contain are lethal. Even dogs and cats are susceptible if they ingest certain plants in the allium family. The allyl methyl sulfide your body produces after you eat garlic is thought by many to ward off mosquitoes and possibly other pests as well, such as fleas, ticks, and barflies. Garlic spray is easily made by running a cup or so of garlic through a food processor with just enough water to help it mill, and grinding it fine. This is a chance to use up small cloves and scrap; no need to peel. Add to a quart of near-boiling water, stir well, and let cool. When cool, strain through a coffee filter and apply liberally with a hand sprayer. I do not add soap, as it tends to mask the pungency. The fresher the garlic, the better. Extra bulbils work fine too.

• **Onion Repellent:** When I came across this recipe, I had to give it a try, but I'm not sure if it is a better repellent or fertilizer. Save onion or other allium trimmings or waste until you have a quart or so, then dump them into a bucket, add a couple of quarts of water, and let it go bad for a week or so in the sun. Strain the liquid and spray the plants you want to protect. Bury the pulp. The originator of this fetid concoction said it was for houseplants as well, but not in my house! It did seem to drive aphids off rose bushes, and it is claimed to be good for spider mites. The same source recommended a similar concoction that comprised one large onion, one button of garlic, and hot peppers finely blended with a half cup of water, added to a gallon of hot water and steeped for a day, and then strained. It is claimed to be a good spray for thrips, aphids, grasshoppers, and chewing and sucking insects. I would compost but not bury this pulp, as capsicum is not good for worms.

- **Mum's the Word:** As a leading natural source of pyrethrin, the chrysanthemum is easily grown and home-brewed. Most of the world's supply of pyrethrin and *C. cinerariaefolium* comes from Kenya. The USDA, as of 1972, said that synergized pyrethrum is "probably the safest of all insecticides for use in a food plant" and that "a pyrethrum formulation is approved for use around foodstuffs." All pyrethrins are easily hydrolyzed and degraded by stomach acids in mammals, so toxicity following ingestion by pets is very low. However, pyrethrins can be dangerous for cats and fish, and can cause asthmatic reactions in the (rarely) sensitive humans from applying too much of a strong commercial product. Grind the vegetation, leach with tepid water and 1-percent alcohol, strain, and spray.

- **Marigold Plant or Spray:** Depending on the species, marigold foliage has a musky, pungent scent, except varieties bred to be scentless. The scent deters common insect pests, including aphids, cabbage maggots, white flies, and hornworms, as well as nematodes. Tagetes species are often used as companion plants for tomato, eggplant, chili pepper, tobacco, and potato. *Note:* Due to antibacterial thiophenes exuded by the roots, Tagetes should not be planted near a legume crop, as they can kill the beneficial nitrogen-fixing microbes the legumes host. Some of the perennial species are deer, rabbit, rodent, and javelina resistant. Leaves, roots, and seeds are finely milled and leached with hot water for a hand-applied spray. Dry seed heads may also be milled and used as a dust.

- **Tomato and Potatoe leaf mix:** The leaves of tomato and potato plants are poisonous to humans and to some insects as well. Obviously they

do not affect tomato hornworms, flea beetles, or Colorado potato beetles, but they can be toxic to pests that attack other edible plants, such as grasshoppers and white flies. Simply crush fresh tomato leaves, cover with water and steep for a few days, strain, and use as a hand spray. I have read of dried tomato fruit also being used but never tried it on the assumption that if Mikey likes SpaghettiOs so well, the fruit can't really be very toxic.

- **Potato Leaf Tea:** Potato leaves are used the same way, in a ratio of about 1:2. Do not heat, as this destroys the solanine that is the active toxin. Remember that this solanine in potato skins and leaves, although usually destroyed in cooking, is toxic to mammals as well. Potato peelings that show green or have sprouts must not be used even as hog slop: they have killed pen-fed hogs. I have never noticed a bad effect on dumping quantities of potato kins in the compost and have wondered, "Hey, what do they do with the truckloads of skins from factory-peeled spuds?" We have used both the above as foliage sprays on root crops. They are in the same family as tobacco, and tobacco leaves or scrap (or nicotiana flowers) can be used in the same fashion. Specific plant toxins may only affect specific pests.

- **Basil Tea:** Many aromatics that we like, but selected bugs do not, can be more effective largely because they are aromatic. A solution of a cup of fresh, chopped basil leaves dropped into a couple of cups of just-boiled water and steeped until cool and then strained makes a good aphid-deterrent spray.

- **Peppermint Tea:** A packed cup of mint leaves in two cups of water and prepared the same as basic tea above makes a good spray for ants. Because some ants will herd aphids to collect their exuded sugar, a synergistic treatment is to first use basil tea for the aphids and then, when dry, spray with mint tea for the ants; when that is dry, use an allium spray as a mop-up.

Traps and deterrents

Slugs: Slugs can get to be real pests if you do not have free-ranging chickens, and in a secret setting you may not. Although they can raise hob with sprouting plants, leafy veggies, and even bean plants, the good news is, slugs are slow and easy to catch. They are probably the easiest pest there is to trap. Simply set out saucers or ground-level tuna cans of stale beer. Overnight they will come to the scent of the beer, jump in (so to speak), and drown. If you do not keep beer in the house, or if you are unwilling to share, a little yeast in sugar water kept warm until it begins to ferment will work as well. Coffee is reputed to be a good spray for plant leaves versus slugs. My tests were inconclusive. If it works, it may be because slugs die of frustration, from being revved up on caffeine but being unable to move fast. I tried dry coffee grounds around the plant, and it worked about like a ring of sawdust, evidently providing an uncomfortable footing. You can also use wood ashes (if you have acid soil) or finely crushed eggshells. Diatomaceous earth, microskeletons from prehistoric sea critters, works well, even for ants, but I do not favor it as it cuts the innards of earthworms, our soil builders. I once had problems with slugs on bean plants, so I made little rings of some old copper screen for around the bottom

Beer

Japanese beetle

of the stalk. I have since read that slugs will not cross copper wire. The screen collars worked 100 percent, but I do not know if it was because they were screen or because they were copper. Chickens, of course, are a cure for slugs, potato beetles, and hornworms, but if you have only penned poultry and want to bring them a treat, you can trap slugs overnight under an inch of old newspaper, a piece of old carpet, or a board. Slugs are one of the few critters we have found that are attracted to citrus rinds. You can "bait" the above with citrus rinds, watermelon rinds, or banana or potato peelings. If you want to dispatch them in place and don't want to clean your shoe, a vinegar or salt spray will do the trick.

Japanese Beetles: I tried this with mixed results. Mash one banana and mix with 2 cups water, half a cup of sugar, and half a cup of wine. Add half a teaspoon of cake yeast, mix well, and put in the sun in a plastic margarine tub to ferment for a day. Set out in the garden where you have seen Japanese beetles. I did not get Japanese beetles but did get a lot of slugs I did not know were there. Maybe I should have used sake instead of Mad Dog 20/20.

Mosquitoes: You'll never get 'em all, but mosquitoes are easy to trap, and every one you trap, you've prevented from laying a bazillion eggs. Take plastic drink bottles, discard the cap, and cut in two right at the start of the cylindrical part. Invert the cone-shaped top into the bottom like a deep funnel, and secure with tape. Paint the bottom a dark color and fill about a third with water. It works like a flytrap: they fly in but don't seem to find the hole to fly back out. They are attracted to the warm moisture and fly in to lay eggs. Place these traps all over. As an added attractant, add a yeast and sugar solution, which ferments, and the carbon dioxide generated attracts the mosquitoes—just like you do. The most effective mosquito traps, by far, use a fan if you can rig one.

Ants and Mice: Ants will eat cornmeal, which they cannot digest, and will even take it back to the hill for others to eat and not digest. I read one account by a guru saying it makes them explode, but I doubt that, even with popcorn. However, both ants and mice will eat flour mixed with plaster of paris (calcium sulfate), which will set up after they eat it and kill them.

Soap or oil sprays

Recipes abound for plant sprays using vegetable or mineral oil, water, and liquid soap or detergent. Most I have tried did work for aphids, but a consideration here is to remember that most plant leaves breathe from the bottom side of the leaf: do not choke it off with oils. Such sprays are recommended for aphids, codling moth, leaf roller, mealybugs, scaled insects, and white fly. A spray made from Neem soap (from the Indian neem tree) has microbicidal effects. A simple spray of an ounce of Epsom salts (magnesium sulfate) in a gallon of water is a good treatment for black spot, mildew, wilt, and rust. A side benefit is that tomatoes love a shot of magnesium about the time they begin to flower, and if your green leafy veggies are yellowed, magnesium perks them right up, as the magnesium helps with the production of chlorophyll.

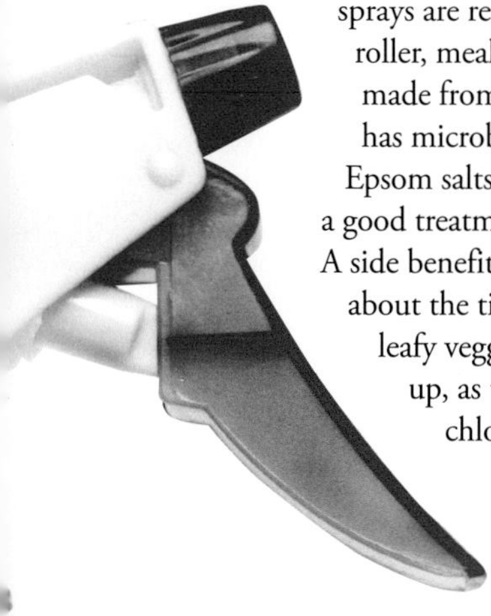

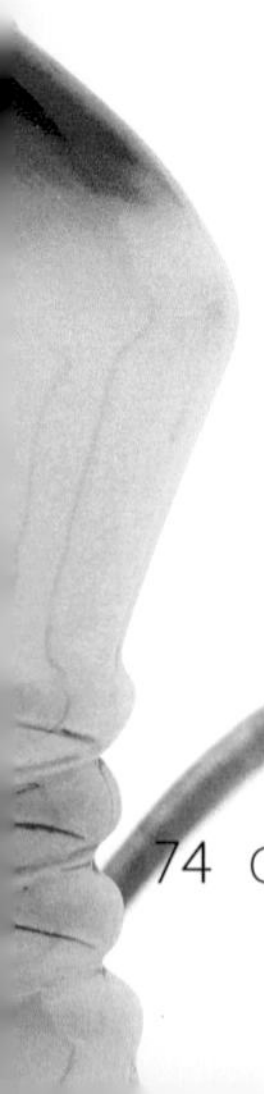

Passive Protection via Hiding & Camouflaging

THERE ARE AS MANY APPROPRIATE TECHNIQUES for hiding crops as there are settings. We have discussed the techniques of forest gardens, which have various benefits in addition to not looking like a purposefully planted agricultural plot.

Real crops can also be hidden among true weeds on genuinely fallow ground, in particular the common weeds that also provide very good nutrition that you can often forage. In this case one merely ups the potential for profitable forage, such as for purslane, dandelion, Jerusalem artichoke, mallow, and similar plants discussed in Chapter 3. The potential is often just as strong, however, for successful commingling of regular, everyday crops among the weeds in a fashion where they blend in.

The technique, once suitable soil conditions have been found, is to plant "groceries" that have a size, structure, and color not dissimilar to what is already established there. The weeds, woods, and fencerows can hide a surprising proportion of crop plants without losing their weed-patch demeanor. Think tomatoes among the pigweed, dwarf corn among tall grass, small plants in the clover fields, compact fruit cukes or squash along fencerows. In every instance, of course, opt for the least-traveled setting.

Is there an abandoned manure pile behind that fallingdown barn, chest high with lamb's quarters, pigweed, and cocklebur? Think bush beans, tomatoes, and similar crops of that size. Often at the edge of such a setting, native curly dock or similar leafy weeds will hide your crops of beets, chard, or kale. Earthworm activity may well have created friable soil near there, suitable for carrots, beets, garlic, and onions. You get the idea: Not everybody will have access to an abandoned barn, but adapt the principle to the site(s) you have.

If you are gardening on public or "borrowed" land, aside from choosing a site in a little-traveled area, be sure to maintain its "nobody bothers to go there" demeanor when you go there yourself to plant, tend, or harvest. Approach and leave by as many different routes as there are.

Consider how a site might look from the air. Are routes to it or trails near it discernible from the air? If you are likely to meet others going in or coming out, you don't want to be carrying visible tools or harvested produce. You should carry no more than what will fit into a well-worn backpack, as might be carried by a survivor just on the bum. If you encounter others, take the initiative: ask them if they have anything they can spare.

The principle of hiding and camouflaging, of course, is that neither has to be somewhere off your own established spot or even outdoors.

"Hidden" buildings

Even an obviously derelict, falling-down barn would not look out of place with a few haphazard, translucent fiberglass roof panels. Especially if south facing, one 2x8-foot translucent panel will provide a surprising amount of light for growing plants if they are not too far from it. In an overt "Yup, I live here" urban or suburban setting, translucent roof panels or even walls are common on garden sheds, and they in effect can be a greenhouse if appropriate junk is left next to the walls to be seen from the outside, and an appropriate level of neglect is obvious around the outside.

Existing smaller structures from a coal chute to a basement window well can be converted to a cold frame, sunheated with a glass or plastic lid, easily covered when necessary with a pile of derelict plastic lawn chairs, worn-out plastic tarps, or similar opaque but light effluvia. A "hot frame" is essentially the same structure but naturally heated by a deep layer of decomposing manure in the bottom. Reconnoiter your spot for such sites and for camouflage trash that will look at home there. In my case, that is seldom a problem.

Junk per se may be a suitable cover for secret plants. I once stumbled across an abandoned collection of semi-antique car bodies stacked on end to hold a sandy riverbank in Arizona, inside of which had apparently been planted a lot of illicit herbs.

Dedicated structures can vary from a small raised bed with a bow-type cover to a large semi-subterranean hothouse, such as a walipini or a converted swimming pool. Coverings for such things can be built from a variety of materials—read: whatever you have—but one of the best suppliers of covers for such things is DeWitt and Co. (www.dewittcompany.com). Its N-Sulate products are visually opaque from the outside but admit some 80 percent of the sunlight and have very good insulating properties. As a nonwoven fabric, it readily adapts to many configurations, from covering a small raised bed to covering a repurposed swimming pool or a purpose-built walipini. Be sure to add an extra-loose panel here and there to flap in the wind, to make it look derelict from a distance.

A nicely maintained hothouse is pretty much a giveaway that you are growing something, which lessens its appropriateness for clandestine efforts. But there are ways of accomplishing the same thing by doing multiples on a smaller scale.

The walipini has been described as a "pit greenhouse," but the classic ones from Bolivia usually are dug into a side hill, like many old sod houses. The primary advantage of a walipini is its ability to use the earth's natural heat, and when this is combined with the solar advantage of a hothouse-type roof, there is a synergism in the energy saved or gained. The structural advantage of digging into a side hill, as opposed to a four-sided pit, is that in a side-hill location, it is usually easy to drain away water. In a pit, depending on the water table, soil, or other factors, it maybe necessary to depend on pumps to protect against flooding.

Many years ago I saw an 8x12-foot hothouse its owner had simply dug into a south-facing clay bank that lay at about a 30-degree slope. He provided a combination roof/sloping front wall made from poles cut on site and overlaid with clear plastic. He had a drainage ditch above the dugout to turn water coming down the hill away from his hothouse, and a ditch in front that led away any water there—simple, efficient, and very cheap. In a secretive situation, such an installation, especially a series of smaller ones, would not be hard to disguise or hide from a distance. Even one adapted by half-burying a small fiberglass model could discreetly hide in a backyard.

Roof gardening

This can refer to either various types of container or raised-bed gardening on (usually) a flat roof or what is often called a "green" or vegetated roof, which is a productive spinoff of the traditional Scandinavian sod roof. The first one I remember seeing was decades ago in Oregon, where a childhood neighbor had dug his pump house into a side hill and given it a sod roof laid over cedar poles and thick cedar shakes covered by miscellaneous salvaged sheet iron. It had about a 3:12 pitch, common to the area where we did not get a lot of snow but did get a lot of rain. It had enough topsoil on top for a hearty planting of native perennial grasses, just like in Sweden, but the attraction was he had planted strawberries among the grass. Virtually all the roof could be reached by hand, and, as strawberries are wont to do, runners trailed down over the sides as well. It did need a drink of water once in a while in a hot summer, but, hey, it was a pump house.

Ernie had just planted the berries as a lark when his neighbors kidded him about the unconventional roof, but the berries thrived and became his prime source of replanting runners for his garden patch as they trailed over the eaves. Most any perennial plant with a shallow and fibrous root probably would work just as well, even small woody shrubs like huckleberries. One consideration for planting on a roof is that some acid-loving plants produce enzymes or harbor bacteria that break down wood (as in your roof timbers).

Container gardening on the roof is pretty much like container gardening anywhere else but with some unique benefits for a setting that may offer few options. First, a rooftop takes advantage of otherwise wasted space. If it's a multi-story building, such as an apartment, the roof and window boxes may be the only outside growing access there is. Unless your roof has a solar array, it's just something to turn the rain away. For plant growing, a roof provides access to the full sun, usually without interference from shading trees. A rooftop is remote from grazers, such as rodents and ground-based insects. Squirrels are usually not hard to exclude, and birds are usually sensitive to visual deterrents, like low-hanging CDs, discreet rubber snakes and owls, or other visual ploys hidden from man but not from beast. A rooftop garden is less visible from the ground, so it is less tempting to looters or snitchers.

It is also less visible from the ground but more visible from the air, unless the particular architecture lends itself to a camouflaged-from-the-air building, such as a dugout with a split half-sod/half-conventional roof. The downside is that planting media, containers, and water must be hauled to the roof, and the roof must be able to support the weight and either be flat or modified for placing containers and providing access. See Chapters 7 and 8 for information on container and raised-bed gardening for ideas that may work on the roof you have available. And keep in mind the usable space under the roof as well, as in hanging from the eaves, behind skylights in the attic, and other creative options.

Wall and fence gardening

The traditional window box has always been popular for flowers, herbs, and small vegetables, primarily because it sits outside a window that gives access from the inside of the house. The other advantage is that it uses space that otherwise would be wasted. Virtually every wall and fence, therefore, is potential window box territory unless there is reason to keep the wall exposed, such as with a heat-gathering Trombe wall or if there are productive vines being trained up them already. In the instance of a fence, depending on your climate and the sun requirements of the particular plants, both sides might be used, which would help increase productivity and balance the load.

One of the most clever ad hoc, best-practice use of a wall I have seen was a 12-foot retaining wall that had been built at about a 50–60 degree slope of overlapping layers of old automobile tires. It had been so neatly done in the beginning, you had to look at it twice before you realized you were looking at hundreds of nasty old discarded tires. The small exposed crescent at the front of each successive layer had been filled with soil and the original planted with such rooty perennials as St. John's wort and ivy, Russian sage, and iris. It was an attractive and practical retaining wall, and unlike riprap it gave the option for a "living" wall. The current owner was in the process of pulling the ivy and St. John's wort and replacing it with edibles, but I fear he'd never get it all and would be fighting the original homesteaders forever. It would have been much better to have planted something edible originally that could take the heat of the tires. But structurally it was a good system.

I saw a similar application of old tires as a retaining wall that had been completely overgrown with blackberries. Had other edible crops been planted as well, as in the example above, they probably would be safe from casual molestation due to the prickly overgrowth of the blackberries.

This is mentioned here in the context of using overlooked space, in situations where any potentially productive space may be valuable. And it leads us to the next topic, the obverse of dispersed and hidden gardening in the woods and hedgerows—intensive gardening.

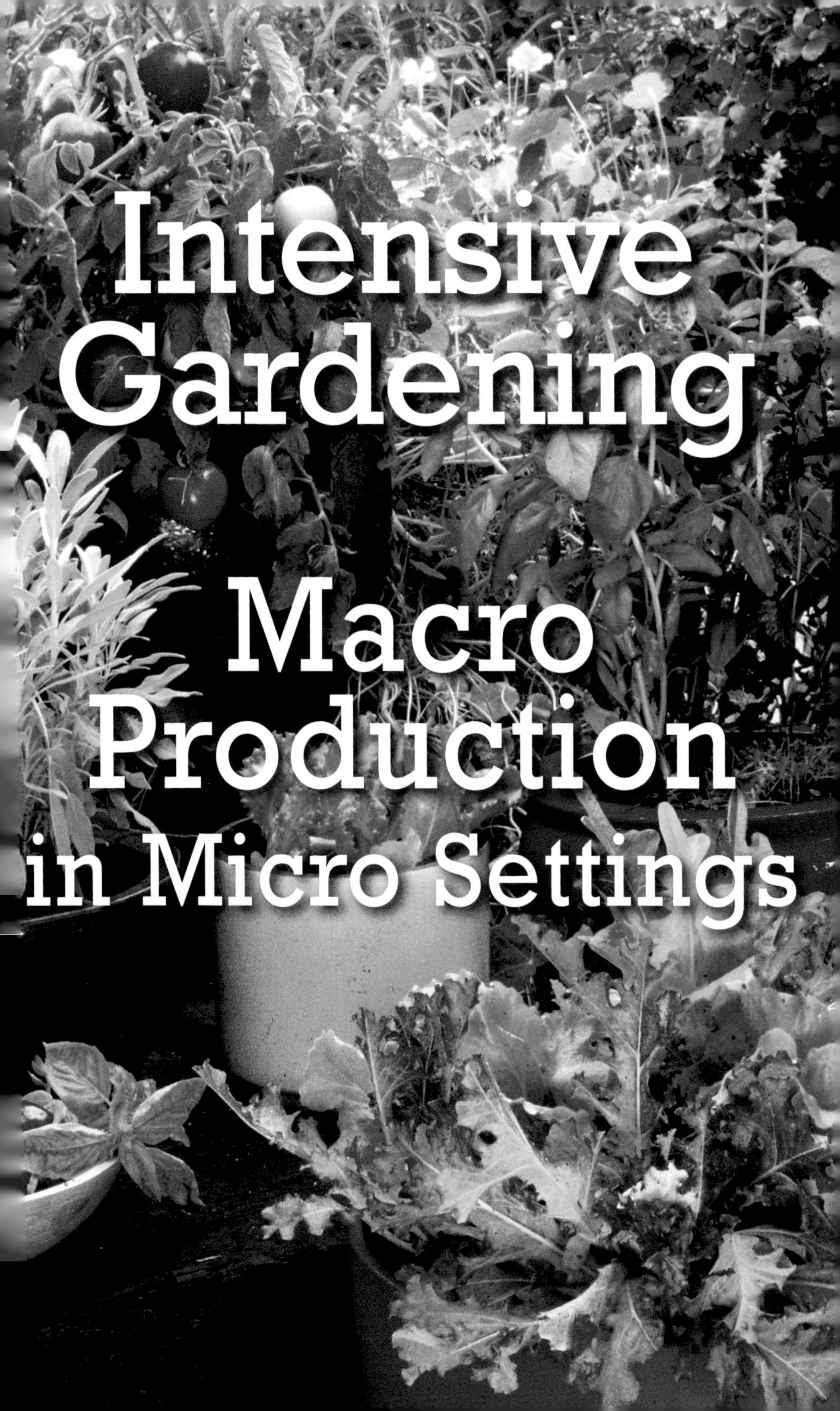
Intensive Gardening
Macro Production
in Micro Settings

THERE ARE MANY TECHNIQUES to accomplish intensive gardening, most of which work with one another to fit your setting. Situations range from little old ladies who grow chives or strawberries in a flowerpot to no-space-wasted hot houses, walipinis, or plots. One outfit advertises plans and instruction courses for its system that can feed a family of four on less than 1/20th of an acre. That's less than a 22 x 24-foot plot to grow all the food one man can eat, which by my experience would have to count on perfect weather year-round, lots of sun, adequate water, great soil, and tubs of Miracle-Gro plant food! But we'll forgive the optimism since they were merchandising a magic plan with the additional promise: "a great garden in any soil—or no soil—and in any climate."

My own plan is pretty simple: you feed the soil, the soil feeds the plants, and the plants feed you. The space a plant needs to thrive is somewhat analogous to the amount of range a cow requires: it depends a whole lot on how good its forage is. The richer the soil, the less of it is required per plant. Below I share what has been done that works and my thoughts on making soil all that it can be, a prerequisite for intensive gardening.

Home Sweet Horticulture

Think back and remember those old folks you liked to visit as a kid. Every flat spot in their house had a plant sitting on it, didn't it? And every windowsill. Decorative houseplants probably would not be granted such prime real estate in hard times, but the point is that if you have a house, from a hogan to a Winnebago to a mansion, the controlled climate inside and the compact handiness of it all make a great environment for growing food. It can range from herbs, sprouts, or a strawfilled wastebasket can of spuds to large containers of a wide variety of veggies. Such legal crops can take advantage of every window, and something will grow anywhere there is daylight. Some do not even require daylight. And if you crave something pretty and just have to have flowers, don't forget such edible ones as nasturtiums, geraniums, violets, and pansies.

In general terms, compact, shade-tolerant vegetables of any kind are suitable for growing indoors. Arrange them for efficient tending or harvesting, and think vertical. You will be surprised at what all you can grow just on a repurposed bookshelf in front of a window. I have seen a bean tipi planted under a skylight in an unused upstairs room that rivaled anything grown in a hothouse. Basement window wells can readily be covered with rigid plastic bubble covers or something homemade and become prime all-season growing country as well. Indoor plants, like all plants, like consistency. Stable temperatures in the 60s and 70s, consistent lighting, and regular watering are all beneficial for indoor plants, edible or decorative. Some decorative

plants are manipulated by controlling light, fertilizer, water, and other factors into a particular mode you want, like chemically "forcing" blooms, starving poinsettia plants for light to turn colors, or similar machinations. I don't particularly like this kind of abuse, as the poor plant is just trying to survive, like anybody else.

Windowsills and window boxes

Windows come to mind because they represent the sunlight that most plants need. Window gardening may provide the easiest access to small crops without having to leave the house. Window crops may be a good place to start if you are not yet addicted to growing your own food, and they can provide easy harvests while you tool up in a serious way for bigger things.

Windowsills: Simply trading the geranium that's already on the windowsill for a pot of herbs or edible greens can get you started. Any window is better than no window, but most windowsill crops like six hours or more of sunlight a day. Most will grow OK with less but will probably become "leggy," as in more stem and less foliage, as they work to find more daylight.

Herbs and seasoning greens are handily grown on a kitchen windowsill because they are right where you need them, so you can pick and choose and

waste nothing. Kitchen windowsills are also a great place to start seeds, as they are in your field of vision and the water they need is right there. Herbs that do well on a windowsill include parsley, tarragon, basil, mint, thyme, oregano, and rosemary. Nutritional crops that do OK on windowsills include salad greens, wheatgrass, chickpeas, beans, and other sprouts, and even dwarf cayenne peppers. Herbs are better if the soil is a little lean, but for food crops give them some of your best. Avoid the tendency to overwater. Because of the single source of light, plants should also be turned a bit every few days so they grow evenly. That's easy for pots, but if you have them in space-efficient long containers, turn them 180 degrees every week or so. In he winter, if there is frost on your window, remember that these plants' microclimate is getting cold as well. If they touch the glass, expect some frost burn.

Window Boxes: A window box can be mounted either outside or inside to take advantage of extended warmth, or do both where you can. An exterior window box can be as big as you can safely hang, while an interior box usually has to fit within the window opening, unless there happens to be nothing on the wall on either side. As noted previously, shelves of your design can fill the light from a window with plants of your choice. If you have a floor-to-ceiling window, think in terms of a floor-to-ceiling shelf setup. Commercial windowsill or exterior window boxes are available, but it's been my experience that they are expensive, not strong enough, and usually unavailable in the configuration you want. An unstable box, however, can have a stronger box built around it, and as they are invariably synthetic, they do well to contain the water. Square plastic food containers can be cut down and fit into a stronger wood box. Small containers inside a larger, waterproof box can be handy, as they let you rearrange the plants with little disruption of their neighbors. Square tubs, like the containers that cat litter and laundry soap come in, can be easily cut down for watertight inserts for your own wooden box, but many are strong enough to not need it. A "greenhouse window" (think of it as a storm window that has more depth to it) can extend the shelf space of a window without being too noticeable from the outside. Such additions can double, or more, the inside potting space of a typical window.

Making niches and inches productive

If you have little obvious space available, container techniques for gardening in restricted spaces are worth exploiting because there are so many wee spots that are not obvious to the potential gardener or potential marauder.

Any built-up environment—small lawns, balconies, patios, porches, rooftops, areas in front of windows, or inside the home in any other available place that has light—can host a food plant. The net usable area adds up when it is all used. For instance, plant shelves are not restricted to being in front of a window: they can be to either side as well, as long as there is light.

Bucket Brigade

Socially, the common plastic bucket is toward the low end of raised beds and containers, but as noted earlier, it takes a lot of food to keep a person going. The good news is, if the best space you can come up with is for buckets, just do a lot of buckets. Get chummy with a few fast-foot restaurants or drywall hangers and you will have more buckets than you can use, and they work fine inside or out. I will deal with "containers" in the context of buckets just because they are cheap and one of the most practical and adaptable containers. I don't mean to do this to the exclusion of other containers you may happen to have or like.

Staying Grounded: A generic 5-gallon bucket has a footprint of less than a square foot, so you can stick them all over and anywhere. An additional advantage is, if they are unburied, you obviate a lot of hassles from many varmints and insects. Whether on or in the ground, they will need a drainage hole, of course, but a plant in a bucket will use less water, and bucket rims are adaptable to attaching jerry-rigged watering systems. An additional advantage of buckets is that you can plant early and leave them out late, as they can be moved in and out to accommodate climate changes, such as frost, or relocated to take advantage of the best seasonal sun or rainfall. And, yes, a light-duty hand truck really does help because some of these plants can get very heavy, especially late in the season.

Inverted Planting in Buckets: Buckets can also be hung from the eaves or porch, and you can invert plants and grow them from the bottom of a bucket, including full-size tomato plants. So think creatively. One time, just for grins, I made horizontal slits in a plastic bucket, softened the material above and below the slits with a torch, and then formed them into small pouches. I had everything from strawberries to radish plants hanging in buckets under the eaves.

I should note, though, that root crops thus grown are harder to harvest unless grown on top of the bucket. And I'll restate the obvious: Eaves-hanging buckets can be heavy and thus require suitable framing and strong hooks to hold them, and hanging them or bringing them to the ground for harvesting requires a certain level of strength. Further, the plastic buckets of commerce do not have an indefinite life in the sun and will eventually degrade to the point where they are no longer safe to hang. You do not want a heavy bucket of soil to fall and crush what is below it. You know, like a gardener.

Crops that are often started indoors and transplanted after the last frost all did well growing out the bottom of a bucket: tomatoes, peppers, and small squash, such as acorn and zucchini. The simplest way to retain the transplant until it gets established, since you need a hole big enough to either get the plant's roots or the tops in through the holes, is to cut a big enough hole and then dress around the hole with a coffee filter or a piece of old sponge or foam rubber with a hole and a slit from the side to that hole. Once the dirt settles, new roots hold the soil in place. Overwatering, of course, can wash the soil, and a small plant or new seedling, out the bottom hole.

Top crops that you usually plant in the ground, like peas and bush beans, did OK in the side pouches. I tried kohlrabi in side pockets, but the weight of the edible portion bent over and choked the roots, so the results were mediocre. Beets, onions, cabbage, and carrots all did fine planted right side up in a bucket whether it was hung for want of space or sitting on the ground or a rooftop. On the theory I was giving them good homemade soil and all they lacked were water and sunshine, I did a number of double-dip plantings with plants both growing out the top or bottom and in side pockets. It would be fun to try any combination, but these grew fine:

- **Beets on top, beans in the pockets**
- **Beets on top and cukes in the pockets**
- **Carrots on top, tomatoes out the bottom, and purslane in the pockets (looked like a chia pet gone crazy)**
- **Carrots on top, tomatoes out the bottom**
- **Garlic on top, peas in the pockets**
- **Tomatoes out the bottom and beans in side pockets (hard to harvest one from the hanging jungle without disturbing the other)**

I have seen the small cherry-type tomatoes grown in Europe in upside-down, 2-liter pop bottles held in netting, with their bottoms cut out. I have also seen fresh herbs grown in the same way and nailed along a wood fence. Every surface with light can be used to grow something!

Who Likes Buckets?: Not all, but most, food plants can be grown in buckets, even dwarf varieties of woody shrubs. Even ones you might not think would grow in a container can often benefit from such trade-offs as less risk of soil-born diseases, virtual freedom from weeds, and the easier control you have over moisture, sunlight, and temperature, particularly if the buckets are mobile. The single-biggest gain may be that you can completely control the makeup of the soil.

Unless it is the foliage itself you want, look for bush or dwarf varieties. Four to six inches of soil in a container can suffice for leaf greens, Asian greens, mustards, garlic, radish, basil, cilantro, thyme, mint, and marjoram. Eight- to 12-inch-diameter pots are ideal (a generic bucket is usually about 12–13 inches) for beans, beets, chard, carrots, cabbage, pepper, eggplant, tomato, squash, rosemary, parsley, lavender, and fennel. Salad greens and some herbs have shallow, fibrous root systems and are well suited to shallow containers with a large surface area. I have had good luck planting the smaller ones as a companion crop in a larger bucket. Purslane is excellent for this purpose and, in a well-fed, well-tended bucket, will lavishly cascade over the sides. Thus I feel a little overkill on pot size (e.g., bucket) and volume can also vary based on the crop, although many feel that 1- to 3-gallon containers are adequate for herbs, green onions, radishes, onion, chard, pepper, dwarf tomato, dwarf cucumber, and basil.

I prefer 5-gallon size for regular tomatoes, cucumbers, eggplants, beans, peas, cabbage, and broccoli. All these vine crops will want support unless they are planted out the bottom of a hanging pot. This is one instance where the el cheapo hardware-store wire "tomato rings" actually are useful, as they fit down inside a bucket. Even laths or branches driven down the side of the bucket are helpful.

After harvest, give the bucket a shot of good compost and plant a new vegetable in it, which will be happy with the new seasonal weather. Plants in the cabbage family do well in colder weather. Note that plants in a bucket will freeze more quickly than ones in the ground ... but you can move the bucket inside at night until you get tired of it.

Few plants, except for ones that usually grow in a swamp (like taro or lotus), are happy with wet feet. Any container must have soil that will drain well, as well as a place for it to drain. A drain hole is a necessity for any bucket on or in the ground. Alternatively, you can fill the bottom of the bucket with 6–7 inches of gravel so the water has a place to go, and then be disciplined about your watering. More houseplants are killed by overwatering than by underwatering, and this is probably true of anything in a container as well.

Choosing Buckets: Be careful of containers with dark colors, as they can get hot in the sun, unless this is what you want to happen in very early plantings. There are some very good but pricey paints made to adhere to polyethylene and other synthetics, but our experience has been it's more cost effective to just use cheap paint and replace it as needed. A middle course that might work is to use a very thin layer of purpose-made plastic primer, and put the cheap paint

of choice over that, but we never got around to trying that. Light, neutral earth tones do not stand out the same way stark white, yellow, bright blue, or green do, so this is a consideration for buckets that are not going to be buried.

Be mindful of what was in the bucket before you got it. Food-grade buckets present no problem, nor do cleaned-out buckets that held drywall dope or plaster. Any that held adhesives have to be completely dried; some adhesives (linoleum paste, for instance) are not waterproof and so must be thoroughly cleaned before using the bucket to grow food. Buckets that held chemicals are such a mixed bag, they all would be second choices as they would have to be evaluated individually. Ones that had petroleum products have to be completely cleaned, which is a hassle. Metal buckets do not last more than a season or two unless lined and not buried, and galvanized buckets are likely to add unhealthy amounts of zinc, especially if used to grow tomatoes.

Other Containers: Containers of terra cotta or concrete will dry out faster than synthetic or metal containers. Glazed ceramic containers of suitable configuration work well, but they are heavy and fragile.

A lot of commercial "containers" for plants are made more to sell than to use—that is, they are attractive but dysfunctional. The common failing is they are top heavy, tapering downward like some takeoff of a Grecian urn. Because the perimeter of the bottom is small, you have lost exponentially the soil-holding capacity of the container—in addition to such a small base being unstable.

The soil that goes in the container—"growth medium" to you yuppies who probably own garden gloves—can be tailored to what you plan to plant, as far as pH, nitrogen, and mineral content. It's hard to go wrong with a classic compost that was built with vegetable matter, animal waste, and native soil and then pH balanced for your specific purpose. There are many soil-less mixtures for sale, usually based on vermiculite or peat moss; these can be good because they promote drainage. I just use coarse sand in with the compost. As for the results you will get from what comes in a bag, you'll have to talk to the man who sells it for information on that. I have had, at best, mixed results.

Replanting a root-bound plant is only a problem with the few perennials you are likely to have in a bucket-size container. Cut-down plastic barrels will host a surprisingly big dwarf tree. If you have a generous supply of plastic barrels and can cut them about a foot or so high, they make for a quick and good larger container, as you scale up from a container garden to the raised-bed gardens we will look at next. Discarded kiddie pools, watering troughs, bathtubs, concrete laundry tubs, toilet tanks, and the like all are serviceable growing containers, and some of them help contribute to the tacky ambiance of a place that obviously has nothing worth stealing!

Containers don't have to be just repurposed items; they can be purpose-built from scrounged materials such as construction scraps, and old pallets. One technique for building containers from wood, such as window boxes or specific-size planters, is to always line them with heavy plastic or tar paper to prevent contact between the wood and soil. The soil contains microbes that break down the wood, and if the microbes cannot contact the wood, this is far less apt to happen.

I built several freestanding flower boxes some 28 years ago, from scrap hemlock 2x4s; they had about 2x2-foot inside dimensions. I stapled tar paper ("roofing felt") inside as a liner when I built them but have used no other kind of preservative except several exterior coats of paint over the last three decades. They have been in constant use, holding a succession of flowers or tomato plants every year, and they're still in service with the same tarpaper inside and good for as long as they can

hold a coat of paint outside. Point is: keep wood out of the dirt unless its mulching on down is part of your plan.

The classic redneck repurposed planter is an old tire or a stack of old tires. From small ones to large tractor or truck tires, they can be cut and turned inside out to make a tulipshaped planter for flowers or veggies. They make good ad hoc compost bins or vegetable planters simply stacked up. They're particularly handy for growing spuds: spade the soil and lay the calloused seed potatoes a few inches inside the tire, about 6 inches apart. Cover with a few inches of soil; when the plants reach the top of the tire, add another tire and more soil, and keep doing this as long as you can keep the stack stable. It helps to start with larger tires on the bottom. Three to six tires usually works about right.

When the spuds first bloom, you can go prospecting for new potatoes to cook in a cream sauce with thinned carrots. You can fill the successive tires with leaves and grass as well as soil. In the fall when the plants die back, kick over the pile, pick up your spuds, and store them for the winter. Store them in dry sand in total darkness. If any spuds are green, set aside to cut, callous (surface-dry a day or two), and plant next year. *(Do not eat green potatoes: the amount of solanine they contain is toxic and probably more than would be broken down by cooking!)* Because a stack of black tires draws heat from the sun, you can crowd the planting season some.

Tires are known to leach zinc, a consideration for such plants as tomatoes and cukes, which are good at picking metals out of the soil.

A good crop for tires, for the same reasons of warmth and easy harvest, is the sweet potato. About midwinter, stick a sweet potato's pointy (root) end down in water, and when the sprouts (slips) grow a few inches long, break them off and stick them in water. They will send out roots. Then transplant them to wee pots, and come the last frost you plant them in a low stack of tires filled with sandy, arable soil. They like to be at least a foot from another plant, which limits you to two or three per tire ring, and their vines grow all over the place. Where vines trail on the ground, they'll also grow more roots if they like the soil. Plant at the edge of a garden, or a remote spot, as they'll take over. They like soft, sandy soil, and it can be poor soil as long as it's not hard. You'll typically need about three frost-free months. Pull the vines or knock over the tires after the first light frost. The plants can go feral in the right climate and soil.

One final free-shot at building a raised bed is to use 8x8x16-inch cinder blocks. Stack them two high and as wide and long as you like, and you have a 16-inch raised bed that you can move next year if you want. You can, of course, fill the large holes with soil and plant in them as well, and this helps to keep the blocks in place. Spending a little time getting the footing level and straight can result in a very professional looking job; conversely, you can build it Dadaist and have it look like somebody started to build an outhouse and never got it done, and it probably just has weeds in it.

Vertical (Tower) Gardening

A natural evolution of the traditional strawberry barrel is a large-diameter synthetic pipe (generally 6–12 inches in diameter), mounted vertically, with access for plants along its full length. Most synthetic pipe is thermoplastic, so you can readily warm it with a hand torch and shape it. The most practical height for such a plant tower is about 6–8 feet, but that can depend on what you were able to scrounge.

Having decided how you want to keep it upright (e.g., make a footing, tie it to a wall or pole), the actual "building" is simple. Merely cut slits about a quarter of the circumference, at right angles to the pipe, at the spots you plan to insert a plant. Then heat-soften the top part just above the slit and push it in well; heat the bottom of the slit and gently pull it slightly outward. This forms an elliptical horizontal pocket into which you place seeds or seedlings. Note that you keep the hand torch moving and only heat the pipe to the point that it can be shaped; if you heat it to the point it starts to actually melt and get gooey, you won't be able to control the shape it takes, and it's just a bit away from catching fire.

You fill it from the bottom up by pouring soil or potting mix in from the top. To prevent it all packing down at the bottom, don't make the tower too high. You can also stuff strips of cotton or untreated burlap, or tree moss or coir if you have it, down the pipe every so often, and hold that wad in place with a nail or stiff wire through a horizontal hole.

That strawberries do well in such a contraption is a given, but this also makes an environment for a surprising variety of top crops, from herbs and greens to tomatoes. Many root crops do well, too, but you may find you have built a boat in the basement when it comes to getting a large beet out of a small hole. One consideration is to keep the load balanced: for example, a healthy tomato on one side needs one on the opposite side.

This technique is commonly used in rooftop gardens or wherever you have a small corner in the sun. These types of gardens are easy to maintain once you get the rhythm of watering down. Water judiciously from the top down, by slowly pouring water into the pockets. It works best to have plants with similar water and soil requirements in the same tower. Be sure there is a place for excess water to drain.

A similar technique is to hang a series of pots on a central rod or pipe, spacing as is appropriate for the anticipated plants. The one time I saw this done, there was considerable trouble with a pot breaking, which then could not be changed out because it had other pots above and below it. But it is schematically a good idea, so it might work with the right components.

Raised-Bed
&
"Square-foot"
Gardening

The soil comes to the gardener

Growing plants in beds above ground level makes them easier to plant, tend, and harvest. Soil tends to be looser and more fertile, draining better in a raised bed, which gives access to nutrients by the roots. Soil structure and drainage and tilth benefit a great deal because a raised bed simply does not get walked on and pounded into adobe. For this reason, scant tilling is usually necessary in a raised bed, just like in a Ruth Stout no-till mulch garden. Growing in raised beds can also help get a good start where the native soil does not meet the requirements of selected plants. I say "get a good start" because it has been my experience over the past half century that you can build topsoil as deep as you need or care to. I just left a place where I started with hard, yellow, ceramic-grade clay and 25 years later had dark topsoil full of worms down past two feet in most areas of the garden.

Square-foot gardening

Advocate Mel Bartholomew popularized the term "square-foot gardening" in the early 1980s. Bartholomew has written a number of books and appeared on various television shows, and he maintains a website on the subject. Although a tad stylized for my tastes, his ideas incorporate many mainstream raised-bed techniques, and he has a considerable following among those who prefer to follow a guru. Most of the techniques he espouses for order and arrangement of a garden can be useful in intensive gardening as long as you don't get too wrapped around the axle over making your food patch mimic the geometry of a formal French garden. Thoughtfulness and order, you bet; making it all like it should have a flagpole and an antique cannon in the middle of it, not so much.

Square-foot gardening is a rather stylized permutation of other gardening methods with raised beds. Both use a raised bed, which has a number of benefits. The premise of squarefoot gardening is to have a raised box of equal length and width and divide this box into 1-square-foot areas; the original design was to be 6 to 8 inches deep with 4-foot sides, divided into 16 squares.

Bartholomew (and some other writers) asserts that you need only 6–8 inches of soil and that you should even put down an impermeable layer of something at that point (to prevent weeds from coming up, dontchaknow). And that if you want to grow carrots longer than 6 inches, you should just raise the bed higher in those areas with supernumerary boxes.

I think it is really perverted to disconnect plants from the earth itself. I'm guessing that somebody may have put down a 6- to 8-inch layer of decent soil over hardpan or an old driveway, and when he (or she) didn't find any roots leaving the good soil, he assumed the 6 inches the plants made do with was all the plants wanted. Road apples.

Raised up but still in touch

In the 2 feet of topsoil in my garden, essentially everything except some small herbs would send roots down deep. They did this not just because they could, but also because there was something in their nature that told them to and there was something down there that they wanted. If for no other reason, deep soil is good because the deeper a plant's roots go, the less deadly will be the impact of a drought. Further, many weed plants (e.g., purslane, mallow, dandelion) will actually go way deep in the soil and bring up nutrients for other plants. I once threw my back out trying to uproot a Czech "oak leaf" lettuce plant whose root, when I decided to dig it out with a shovel just to see, went down over a foot.

Sure, I've grown off-season lettuce in 6-inch-deep flowerpots, and it grew pretty well. But that doesn't mean it was happy about it!

Further, the only kind of earthworm you will get to survive in 6 inches of soil is the epigenic red worm, a fine fellow at converting biomass into soil. It works in concert with other species of earthworm that go way deeper, providing deep channels for water and bringing up fresh nutrients for the topsoil. For my money, growing anything in 6 inches of soil is just hothouse gardening without the glass roof. End of rant.

There are many advantages to raised beds, and even some when it comes to planning square-foot gardening that we can use if we keep everything in a less-myopic context. Where I want to plant carrots or spuds, I dig down in the native soil— which is pretty good stuff because the worms have made it so—to make a pocket that is deeper. I also like to plant spuds a little shallow and hill them up with mulch. Another good system for few hills of spuds is as mentioned above: to grow them in a stack of aesthetically insufficient used tires, which is readily knocked over come harvest time.

Benefits of the higher road

To review, raised-bed gardens can be a good idea because they keep you and your big feet off the garden, and in so doing they maintain the soil for easy access to nutrients by the feeding plants. Further, they tend to maintain easy access by Dear Gardener as you plant, tend, and harvest. Pests, crawling or growing, are more easily spotted and dealt with. Because of access and visibility, you can quickly replant behind a harvest, efficiently keep all spots in continual production, and keep mature, or diseased, plants or parts removed.

A raised bed can be planted more closely. Crowding is less of a problem overall than is poor nutrition, drainage, poor soil, inadequate water, or poor sunlight. Closely planted crops tend to self-mulch, hiding the soil surface

Hæmmerlin

from the sun, and losing less water to evaporation. Go ahead and overplant as long as you do not choke out the sun from a plant that needs it. If plants show signs of crowding, eat some of 'em or, if a suitable variety, transplant. An additional advantage of raised beds is that they encourage planning before planting (or changing plans in midstream). This allows you to take advantage of companion crops, or planting short and tall, or top and root crops together, in a strategic juxtaposition. In North America, reserve the north side of a raised bed for planting corn, pole beans, or tomatoes in tall frames.

This easy planning and control is the heart of intensive gardening, which is important when space is limited or you want to limit space as a way to limit visibility. All the principles can be applied, and the benefit derived, without the manufactured/manicured, noticeable aesthetic. Although a square-foot garden imposes a grid on top of the garden to divide it into equal plots that can be used to organize and diversify the plant arrangements (such as a 4-foot square divided into sixteen 1-foot squares), my experience has been that healthier plants do result from intermingling with compatible plants. The idea of an arbitrary grid is a bit claustrophobic, though. If you can't remember that you planted carrots here and beets there, take notes.

The box for a raised bed can be built from what you have, and you don't have to buy specific-dimension pieces to do it. About 4-feet wide is a handy dimension for most folks to reach the middle, and you can make it as long as you want and to meander it to fit the land or space, or to maintain an unkempt aesthetic. Anything that will hold an 8-inch or so bed of dirt will do, although my preference is for at least a foot or two. My first choice in a "regular" garden (as opposed to a hidden garden) is to use a 2-inch-thick concrete wall. It is good forever and is readily made in movable components, or you can pour in situ. The cost, even if you use the more expensive Sakrete for its handiness, is in favor of concrete versus wood unless you have free wood. The 8x8x16-inch concrete blocks are also price competitive with poisonous treated wood, and they are a superior choice and guaranteed forever not to rot, not just for 10 years.

You have probably seen raised beds of varying degrees of sophistication, or photos of them, built of treated, rot-resistant lumber. The most common treatments are chromium or arsenic salts or chlorinated hydrocarbons.

Every treated board has a tag stapled to it warning you that it is poison, not to burn it, and to wash your hands. When you see this used by a guru, just hope he is raising flowers because he is poisoning his tomatoes, and probably his minions, with heavy metals. Use the safe material you have. Free is good: stone, used brick or block, salvaged broken concrete, or untreated lumber.

Before filling the box with soil, some say to place a weed barrier in the bottom. We think this is a bum idea, for reasons already mentioned. Virtually all guru recipes want you to fill these raised beds with something you buy at the store—vermiculite, sphagnum peat moss, plus a blend of various sacked composts. The first two, although pricey, can be good, but I have little interest in bagged compost made from poisoned feed-lot bedding. Rotted sawdust, rotten leaves, or other single-component items do not become compost just because some New York merchandiser stuffs it into a plastic bag. Compost is, by dictionary definition, a mixture of feedstock, coming from the same root word as "composite." When a guru says to blend different kinds of purchased composts to use in his "system" because some compost may only be rotted sawdust, the huckster/promoter alarm goes off, as it means somebody is selling a mislabeled product, and the teacher seems to know no better.

What you have is probably better

Luckily, however, in a hard-times scenario what infrastructure there still is will probably not be engaged in hauling peat moss and poisoned manure around, and such ersatz compost probably won't be available anyway. You can easily make a peat substitute by soaking mulched leaves underwater in a barrel for a year. Vermiculite is a great mineral product but can be exchanged for coarse sand. The compost—you know, the real stuff—is free, and I talk about it in more detail below. Well-rotted cow (think dairy cow, not feedlot), rabbit, and chicken manure is good. Actually, none of it is bad if uncontaminated. You can also compost right in the raised bed and plant in the immature compost. Whenever I have to build a compost pile in the middle of the garden for reasons of space, I build it around a bucket and then pull out the bucket, fill the hole with soil, and plant something nutritionally greedy. Anything that likes a low pH (slightly acidic) soil will thrive. As the plant(s) grow, the pile of mixed ingredients composts down.

Worm castings are excellent for your raised bed, and, of course, worms themselves are wonderful helpers if you leave them with free access to the native soil. An additional point in favor of leaving the bottom of a raised bed in communication with the soil is that when it comes to installing support systems for tomatoes or other vine crops, you need to go into the native soil. Six inches of anchoring in fluffy bedding just isn't going to get 'er done for 6 to 7 feet of happy, heavily laden tomatoes. Mine grow on square trellises made from old bed frame, whose pointed corners pound into the dirt a foot or so. But, then, I've generally gardened for the pantry, not the photographer.

I think you will like raised beds, if for no other reason than it will let you get by another year before you rebuild that carburetor on the tiller. A crowded raised bed really discourages, and actually almost eliminates, weeds and grass among your crops. Rain in this good soil drains more readily. Whatever watering technique you favor, a raised bed takes less of it, and homegrown water systems usually attach well to the raised sides of the beds. The bedded soil warms faster than the ground, meaning that your growing season can start earlier, but it also cools down faster in the fall. A side benefit to a raised bed is that you can readily make lightweight covers from plastic sheet on a frame, and have an as-needed cold frame to extend the growing period of select crops, if you plant with that in mind.

The greatest benefits, though, are effortless control, easy access, and optimization of space. It's up to you if you need to overlay a grid to figure out what you're doing at planting time, but you do need to think ahead about what you will plant or transplant, how much space the mature plant will require, and which ones make good neighbors. If you have a bounty of seeds, feel free to plant "too much" and thin later. Beet thins, for example, are a treat. Radishes come and go so fast they are unlikely to interfere with other plants, and their fast harvest lets you know you do have a garden this year. Planting information regarding timing, depth, spacing, and the like are usually on the packet of purchased seeds. Where the packet specifies "plant spacing" and "row spacing" distances, you can usually go with the plant-spacing recommendation for both ways in a raised bed.

Make sure you site your beds where they will get adequate sun for the crops you anticipate and where you will be able to take advantage of the accessibility. Meandering terraces make a good way to use raised beds in locations where the land is not level. The comfortable access space you leave between adjacent beds is a good place to deposit grass, pulled weeds, or leaves to help diminish soil compaction, and let it mulch down. I would never put anything there that will not break down. If not mulch, then at least plant clover. I have seen poster-child photos promoting a square-foot garden with the kneeling spaces between the geometrically perfect, beautifully manicured beds actually filled with gravel. They must have run out of broken glass!

These paths make good surge reservoirs for mulch you generate but don't

immediately put in the compost. All plantings do better with mulch, but raised beds tend to need less because close planting tends to self-mulch and because raised beds are so handy for mulching with live harvestable crops such as purslane.

Some thoughts on water

Water systems for plantings are going to vary with your crop and climate, and the possible ways to accomplish your job in this regard are uncountable. The obvious does need to be stated, however: your crops will need water, and the time to figure that out is before you select and plant. If you can plant near or below a watercourse, where you can divert small quantities of water unnoticed, go for it. In a permanent situation, catch and cistern setups may provide enough water. Seek out moister spots that appear to be sub-irrigated.

In most situations, however, count on conservation being a continuing effort. And for conservation, mulch is your first line of defense. I prefer natural mulch, as it adds to the soil, but there is nothing wrong if you have it and want to discreetly use plastic sheeting. Container and raised-bed gardens, of course, bring with them an inherent water-conservation benefit, compared to spray or flood irrigation.

In the case of such containers as buckets, no water is lost unproductively to the surrounding soil, the soil in the top of the bucket is readily mulched, and there is an old Indian trick that works well for plants in buckets: soft-fired terra cotta flasks of about 1 quart, shaped like a slender gourd, are set in the bucket. When filled with water, they slowly weep through and keep the bucket hydrated for quite a while; how long mostly depends on what is growing in the bucket and drinking the water. In some places south of the border, they were the old poor-man's canteen, as the seeping water evaporated and kept the flask cool, as does an old cowboy canteen or water bag.

Superabsorbent polymers (SAPs) can absorb and retain extremely large amounts of a liquid relative to their own mass and are used for retaining soil moisture in arid areas. They are now commonly available in garden stores in flowerpot quantities, and their benefit is that they absorb and hold water and do not give it up to evaporation, but they will give it up to a plant. So if you forget to water, your African violet doesn't die. In the early days of America's involvement in Afghanistan, when we were helping the mujahideen in the Soviet War in Afghanistan from 1979–1989, we gave them quantities of SAPs to plow into mudholes on Ivan's tank trails to create tank traps that would never dry out.

As an agricultural amendment for arid-land farming, it has a life span in the soil of about seven years. It can be handy stuff to keep plants alive if you are not there very often to water them. Seek out quantity suppliers, as flower-shop prices are high.

If you're planting in buckets and you have a lot of buckets, you can use a bottom bucket as a water reservoir that wicks its water up to the top bucket through a rag as the soil dries. It entails running a length of PVC pipe through the top bucket and into the bottom bucket to fill it several inches with water, but it saves a lot of watering time and provides a margin of safety if you will not be there to water often. Simply make the hole big enough that the fill tube and a rag will both fit through it.

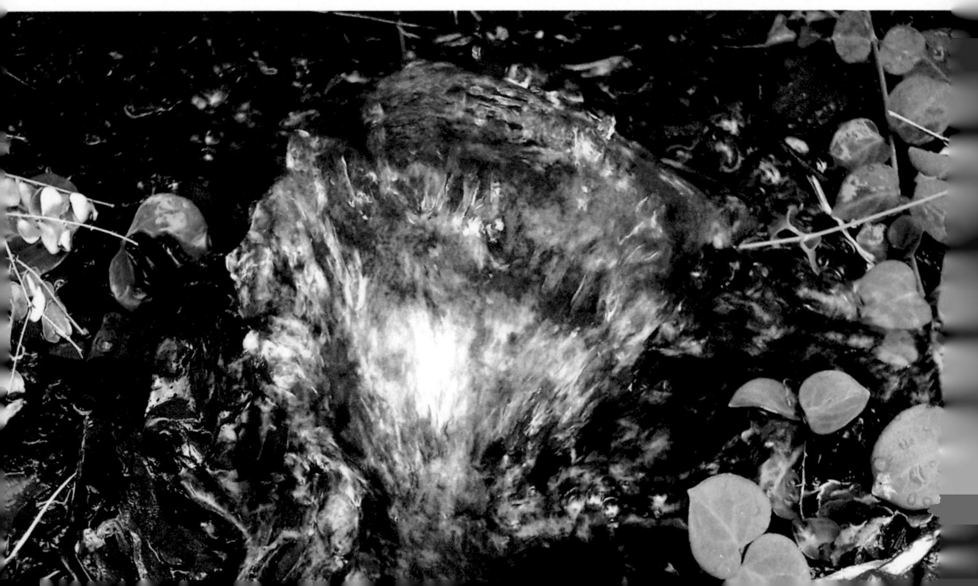

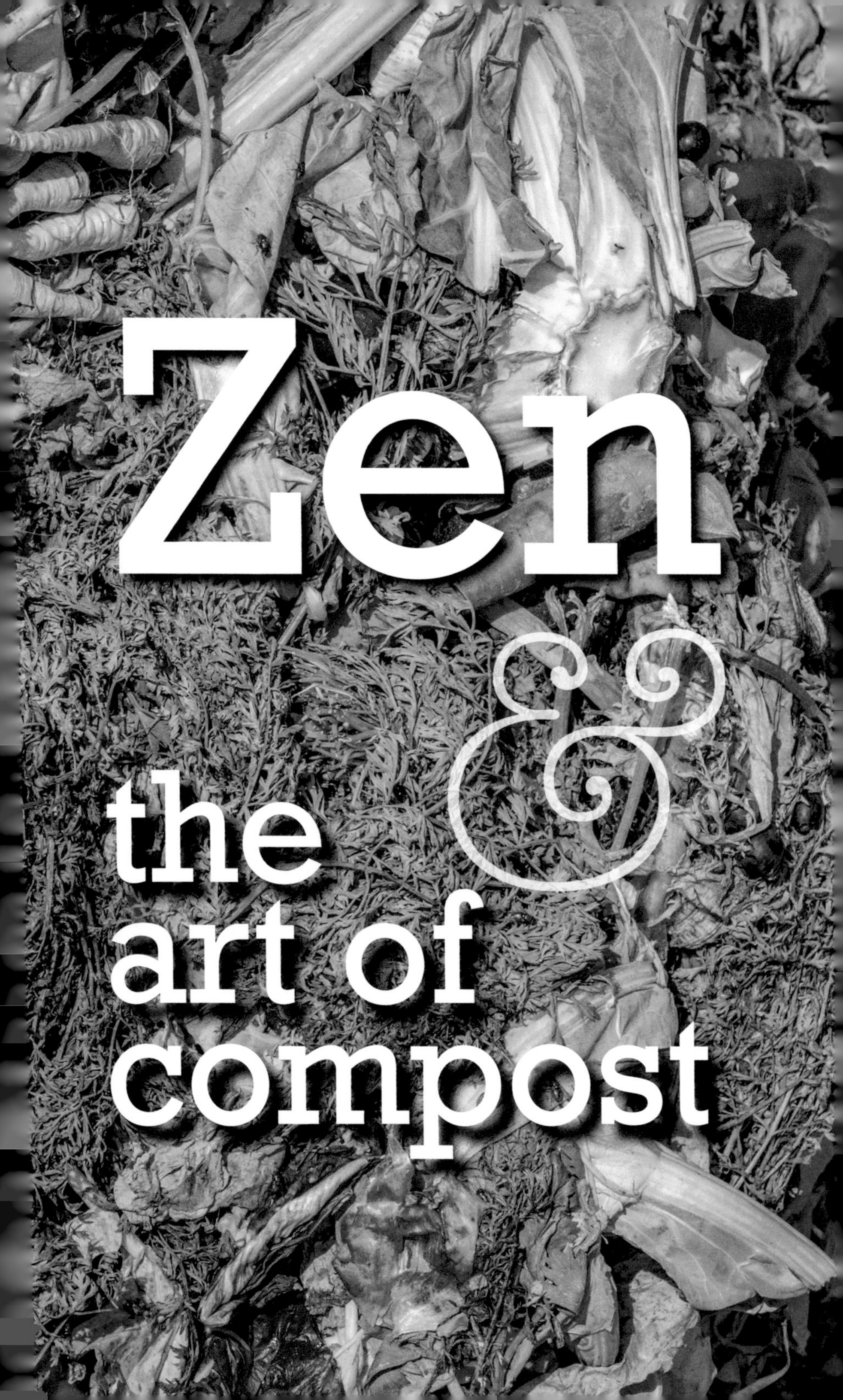
Zen
&
the
art of
compost

Chapter 9

MOST ANY SOIL WILL GROW SOMETHING, but we are dealing with the premise that what we grow will mostly be done in small plots or small containers, or with a small ration of loving care after it is planted. It is in the interests of plant survival for them to be well fed, just as we hope for ourselves and for the same reason.

What a plant grows in, therefore, may be even more important than where it grows. Lucky for you, you have a large measure of control over what your plants grow in, and you do not need any particular agricultural experience to do well by them.

Soil, the most important thing you can grow

Attitude is one of the most important factors in surviving. There is nothing to help your attitude like seeing your own personal garden grow.

It's country simple that you can't get something out of anything unless it has been put in. If you want the plants to feed you, the soil has to feed them. If you want the soil to feed the plants, you have to feed the soil. In the short term, factory fertilizers will grow crops, but in the long term they do not replenish the topsoil of all that is being removed. In a hardtimes situation where you do it yourself or die, the good news is that you can do it yourself the right way pretty much for free. Everything is going

to rot anyway, so use it efficiently to build your soil and container mixes from the ground up.

Nature doesn't waste a thing, and in a natural setting it's a truism that one organism's trash is another's treasure. The carcass or offal from one plant or animal feeds another plant or animal. As part of a carefully planned and complex mechanism, the benefit eventually returns to the original plant or animal species, with all that's needed to keep the cycle going being energy from the sun and minerals that are already there.

We've been smart enough to affect this cycle but not wise enough to always do it for the long term: our short-sighted, "efficient, economically viable" agricultural practices over the past 150 years have starved the topsoil that feeds life on land. We have taken the nutrients we should be putting back into the soil and use them to either pollute the biosphere or take up usable land to warehouse garbage, while at the same time killing or starving microbes and fauna that build and maintain living soil.

It's not that after millennia we have suddenly become stupid, as we have always been capable of grand error—it's just that now we have the technology and machines to really make a mess in a hurry, without even breaking a sweat to do it. Fortunately for a survival garden, we probably don't have the time or space to do it any other way except nature's way, and that's a good thing.

If an independent operator wants to feed the soil that feeds him, on a small to medium scale, the way to accelerate the process is to compost the plant food, as nature does but faster. Then it is immediately usable to the plants and microorganisms that live in the soil and fill our larder.

The cult and commerce of composting

Even on the smallest scale, composting is good news. But the bad news is, when you endeavor to study up on the topic you're led to believe that to compost you either have to join some sort of cult or, at minimum, go to school and read a lot of books, or you have to spend a lot of money. Not true. Composting as such has been practiced since the time of Pliny the Elder. Small and subsistence farmers in Central Europe and Asia were composting before the industrial revolution and have never quit. The thing to keep in mind is that nature has been composting forever, entirely without our help, and is going to keep on composting with or with out our help, and just may decide to compost us as well if we don't clean up our act.

For our purposes it is easy to speed up nature's process and help it in the direction that will serve us individually without soiling the communal nest. There are some common-sense techniques (OK, you green control freaks can call them "rules" if you just have to) to follow, but all you need do is sit on a stump and watch what nature does and then do likewise. It's not all that complicated. And you don't have to let somebody sell you either an idea or a machine to get it done. With a little organization, you can get it done more quickly and get it back into the stream.

Types of composting

There are two basic types of composting: aerobic, which relies on or encourages oxygen-loving microbes; and anaerobic, which relies more on microorganisms that do not need much oxygen, if any. Each type of composting has its uses, and sometimes they are used in sequence to accomplish a specific task or obtain a specific end result. Aerobic is usually more appropriate for small-scale agriculture, unless you are set up to do bokashi fermenting, which greatly speeds up the process.

Types of compost feedstock

If you'd believe what you read, regurgitated over and over by necrophagous writers who have probably never held a shovel, you can only compost "browns" and "greens" and never-never-never can you compost meat, fish, dairy, fats, and oils, even citrus. Well, that's pretty stupid: if they didn't decompose quite well, thank you very much, the Earth would be piled a hundred feet deep in greasy roadkill and orange peels alone. For our purposes here of clandestine gardening, something that looks like a garbage pile is less attractive and, therefore, preferable to a catalog-bought plastic contraption. Further, the excludables listed above are readily buried deep in a garbage pile–style compost heap so they neither smell nor attract vermin. Of course, if a compost operation is purposely left to go sour and smell, that tendsn not to attract vermin of the two-legged type.

You can compost critters too; just bury them deep enough in the soil that other critters and flies won't pursue the carcasses or offal. When it is ready, plant roots will find it when decomposition is complete. In the case of birds scrounging for a few food scraps, note that they poop regularly while there, which I consider a fair trade. You can compost anything that was ever alive, except for coal and petroleum. In fact, if the county coroner ever digs in my veggie patch, I'll probably go to jail!

Having selected what to compost—everything—the how is all reasonable and straightforward. As we already pointed out, things want to go back to the soil with or without our help, so why not help a little and get it back in the soil more quickly? After generations of starvation, the soil may be hungry by now. Remember that true compost is a mixture of animal, vegetable, and mineral that will contain a well-rounded diet for the soil. A bag of rotted sawdust may be great for a rhododendron, but it is not compost.

Aerobic is generally easier

Aerobic feedstock is usually classified as "green" or "brown." Green feedstock may or may not be that color, as the term refers to fresh vegetation that still retains its natural starches and simple sugars and is wont to biologically degrade quickly. Fresh manure is also a "green" compost feedstock, whether or not it has rotted down before. The common denominator among "green" feed is its higher nitrogen content. My favorite manure? Rabbit, hands down. Bat guano is so powerful you have to be careful with it. An additional benefit from rabbit doody from caged animals is that it also contains a great deal of urea. Chicken is excellent, but should be rotted down. Rotted cow is wonderful. Everybody has their favorite, but horse is lower on my Christmas list.

"Brown" feedstocks are those plant remains comprised primarily of cellulose: dried grass, straw, dry leaves, sawdust, wood chips, and bagasse. They are treated somewhat differently because the microbes that would break them down require nitrogen, which they are short on, so you mix them with plants that do have nitrogen, the "greens," or manure.

Thus, when building a compost pile or filling a compost barrel, you layer "green" and "brown" so the pile as a whole contains everything needed except water and mineral, which you add; and oxygen, which you introduce by turning or stirring the mass or even with a pressurized air wand if you're set up to do that.

The complexities (not!) of composting

Some 50 years ago when hard-core composters were thought of as mildly eccentric and Rodale's *Organic Gardening* came in a plain-brown wrapper, the optimum compost pile was prescribed as layers of brown, green, native soil, lime or wood ashes, and manure, plus whatever offal you might have, and then repeated until you reached the height you want. A 4x4x8-foot pile would need old stove pipes inlet into it to let heat escape. I doubt that a compost pile would spontaneously combust like a barn of wet hay because

it is wetter and mixed with noncombustibles, but my mama's handcrafted compost piles would get hotter than your hand could stand. This was on purpose, to kill weed seeds, but vents prevented it from getting so hot it would kill the microbes that were doing the work. Large commercial compost heaps are more liable to get hot enough to smolder and for that reason are periodically wetted down with large fog nozzles.

Under ideal conditions, which included a couple of turnings and attention to keeping it moist, these "artisanal" piles would turn out friable compost ready to use and at a decent pH of 6–7 in a few weeks. If you did not have manure, more green grass would stand in its stead because, after all, chemically speaking, grass is just cow manure with the milk still in it. Even with chicken guts discreetly included, these compost piles did not stink. A healthy compost pile nearing maturity does smell, but with the same

Manure and animal bedding

pleasing aroma as good humus.

Doing it in exactly in the manner above is not necessary, but there are specific benefits. First, keeping the compost mixed with all the oxygen it needs converts the carbs to CO_2, which is plant food: without sufficient oxygen, the carbs convert to methane (CH_3) which is an order of magnitude worse as a hothouse gas and is not plant food, as is CO_2. That's fine in a methane generator when you are converting biomass to methane fuel, but not in a compost pile.

You may read that lime kills worms, which it may under certain circumstances, and this you do not want to do as worms are your best friend as a gardener. However, this has not been my experience, as there would be red worms coming up through a lime layer in a compost pile as soon as the composting was complete and it cooled down. Many commercial growers of earthworms use ground limestone to adjust the pH of their beds. An unkind soul, such as myself, might speculate that somewhere along the line a fellow with a typewriter but not a shovel may have confused diatomaceous earth (DE) with lime and killed his worms with a shot of DE, which looks similar but is composed of sharp, microcrystalline silica and cuts a worm's crop and gizzard—and thus may have started a sub-urban legend. Excessive lime that raises the pH way high is bad for worms, but not lime per se.

The technique, I believe, is to never use so much lime you make the soil alkaline or close to it, as this in itself is hard on worms and interferes with the biochemistry that breaks biomass down so that it is worm food. If a pile or barrel turns sour, a small amount of lime or wood ash in water will sweeten it back up, and that, along with aeration and a little less water, should fix it. The presence of some lime or wood ash calcium in compost is important because it helps the nitrogen to convert to soluble nitrate (a technique developed hundreds of years ago when they would make similar niter beds to generate saltpeter, KNO_3, for making gunpowder). I prefer not to shock the soil with a hot shot of lime or ammonium nitrate fertilizer or anything else: treat it gently like the living, complex mechanism it is.

Eclectic Composting

If you want, compost is an ideal medium from which to introduce all sorts of needed amendments to your soil, be they lime/ashes if you need to raise the pH, or iron filings to increase iron, nitrogen-rich animal waste, or sandy components to help tilth. Just be careful not to introduce anything that will hurt earthworms—they are glad to do your work for you, even turning and mixing your compost as it nears maturity.

If you care to do more than make an esthetically challenged compost pile, one thing to avoid is pressure-treated lumber for bins. Read the label on the end of the board. As noted elsewhere, if it says the wood is treated with

arsenic or chromium salts or with pentachlorophenol, put it back in the pile and go wash your hands. And get some cedar or redwood, or free old lumber or fallen logs: when it rots, plow it in and get more.

Compost Tea

Compost itself is a good example of the old axiom that you get out what you put in. All unpolluted compost is good, but some is better than others for some purposes because of differences in the feedstock.

Unless purposefully enriched with high-nitrogen feedstock—like manure, urine, and animal protein, as one would do in a niter bed whose purpose is to create soluble nitrates— much of the "tea" made from vegetable-matter compost is surprisingly lean in what conventional wisdom would assume is there: in lab tests some held less than 100 parts per million (ppm) available nitrogen and potassium.

Compost tea, however, is still beneficial to most plants but for different reasons than often thought. It is usually made by soaking a 1:3 ratio of mature compost in water for several days. It can be filtered and sprayed on foliage or seedlings, as a local soil drench or root dip, or as a surface spray. Its primary benefit seems to be to suppress various leaf fungi by bacterial competition on the leaf surface, aside from contributing a shot of valuable trace minerals.

With this in mind, you can tailor compost that is intended for use in a tea to fit its intended beneficiary. If it is to be used as a "tonic," most any vegetable matter will suffice; but if it is intended to be used as a fertilizer, then you need to add manure, urine, and wood ashes or similar material for the nitrogen and potassium, and be mindful not to use it too heavily.

Friends Beyond Name and Number

Microbes and earthworms are the soil's best friend and, in turn, yours as well. The two most common worms are redworms, or "red wrigglers," and night crawlers. Redworms are smaller and redder, and will actually go after biomass that has not broken down, just as soon as microbes colonize it. Redworms thus are usually marketed as "composting" worms. You're likely to find them in lower pH soil, manure piles, and up in a new compost pile that is at rest. The other common type of worm is the night crawler, which is much larger and lives on thoroughly decayed vegetation. To get this decayed vegetation, they will actually pull vegetable matter into their worm tubes so it can rot down for them, or dine on the castings of redworms. Worms use microbes in the soil, like we use worms. The castings from redworms and other critters make good feed for night crawlers, who live in tunnels or "tubes" that can go several feet underground. So busy are they, worms can change local ecology, usually for the better for gardeners, but not always for everybody: some released to the wild by "kindly" fishermen are in some areas eating the local wood's duff at the expense of local flora.

Food waste with worms

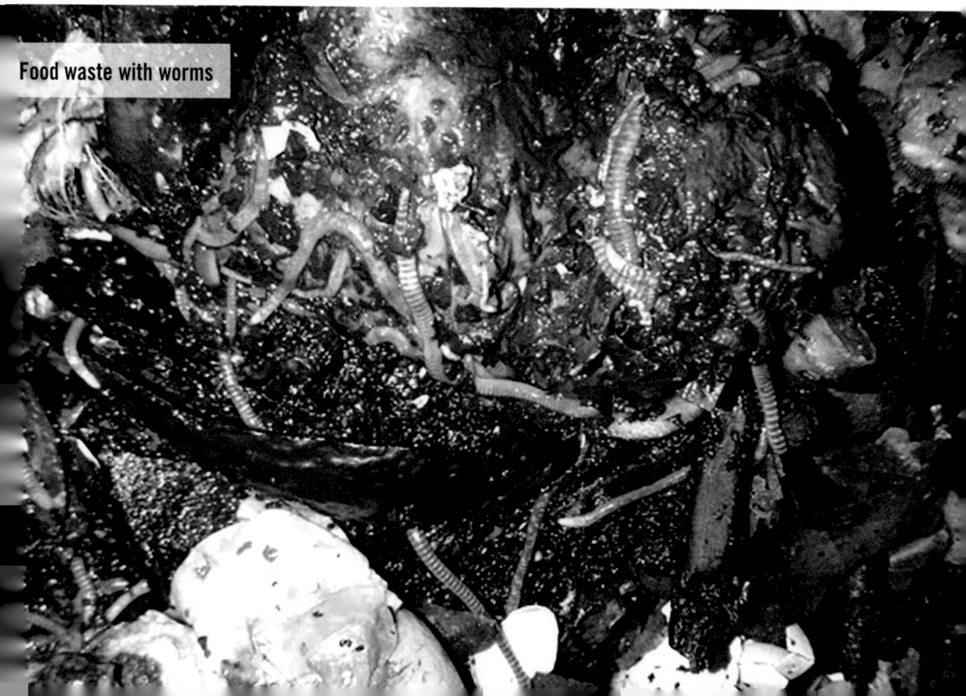

GROWING YOUR HELPERS

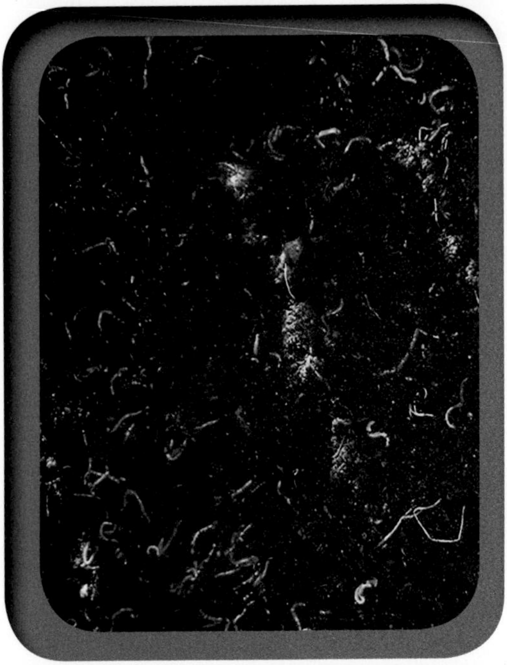

Earthworms readily grow in beds or containers, best in an organized fashion with continuous feeding and mulching, here creating a feeding zone that moves across the bed as biomass is converted to castings.

As biomass becomes rich castings, these are harvested for adding to planting soil, especially containers. Worms and egg cysts can be moved to planting soil as well.

Vermicomposting

This is simply using the right worms as the direct agent for decomposition. It is a parallel idea to black soldier fly larvae mentioned below, but feedstock can be predominantly cellulose or even the final product from growing black soldier fly larvae. You can do it indoors in a small bucket, and if you keep track of what's going on, there is no smell. If you have enough feedstock, 30-gallon (or so) plastic tubs can be used singly or in multiples and generate a lot of worm castings. You can think of worm castings as compost on steroids as for what it will do to enrich soil, and it can be used in the same manner as an amendment or to brew tonic/tea. Containing water-soluble nutrients, vermicompost is an excellent, nutrient-rich organic fertilizer and soil conditioner. These castings contain reduced levels of contaminants and a higher saturation of nutrients than do organic materials before vermicomposting. Worm castings are probably the optimum fertilizer for intensive gardening in small containers. That you produce it by yourself and for free is just a bonus.

Both of the end products, worms and worm castings, are items of commerce, as the worms most often used are of the red wiggler (*Eisenia fetida*) variety, such as is sold in bait shops. They are epigean (shallow dwelling) and feed on decomposing plant matter in the bin. If you are also raising fish or fowl, their feed doesn't get much better than earthworms. They thrive on most decaying vegetable matter and can handle meat and dairy, but these components that are likely to putrefy and draw vermin are better for black soldier fly larvae, or if "pretreated" with bokashi culture.

There are as many "recipes" for growing worms as there are for cooking a stew, but the main considerations are to keep them moist at a moderate temperature, maintain a reliable air supply, and keep them fed. This is easier to do in larger, flat containers, but stacked buckets require less floor space. When their feedstock becomes almost all castings, introduce new material at one end of the bin—they will migrate there, which gives you a chance to remove castings from the other end or harvest worms while they are concentrated. They like the dark. As their name implies, *E. fetida* can emit a defensive foul smell if roughly handled, but they are pretty tolerant of careful handling. If you want to give this a try, either dig some in a manure pile or get a small tub at the bait shop: night crawlers and rainworms who live deep are not what you want.

A worm-bucket setup requires little more than three identical plastic buckets. The bottom one is unaltered unless you want to install a small spigot to draw off the worm juice that collects in it, which is why it's there. Diluted 20:1 with water, it's great tonic/fertilizer for containerized plants. The second and third buckets are identical, with many holes in the bottom for drainage and several holes around the top perimeter for ventilation. Give the worms bedding of grass, leaves, or shredded paper (which they ultimately eat) and food like table scraps. Keep the worms moist but not wet, and cool, and they will usually do fine. When you add more food, lightly dig it into the top material of the bucket. They also do OK on a diet of shredded newspaper only. When the bucket gets full to the point that the top bucket will compress the material, put on the top bucket containing fresh bedding and food and the worms will migrate to that. When they have, harvest the worm castings from the bottom bucket, and the bottom bucket becomes the new top bucket, and so on indefinitely. Harvested worms become new colonies, feed for fish or fowl, or bait.

Enlist a Soldier Fly

One other critter worthy of special mention here is the larvae of the black soldier fly, a harmless little fly that looks like a wasp (its only defense is, in fact, to be a mimic of the organ pipe mud dauber wasp). Black soldier fly larvae are the appropriate omnivorous partners to break down meat, dairy, fats and oils, roadkill, and pig manure, when you have more than incidentals that can hide in a compost pile. Black soldier fly larvae do not carry any known disease of man, and the flies do not invade your house for food because the adult actually has no mouthparts and cannot eat. They hatch, mate, lay eggs, and die. Aside from the diet, that actually sounds like a pretty good life. Only the larvae can eat—in fact, all they do is eat, and they just about eat it all. Their waste is feed for earthworms, their aesthetically challenged little bodies are feed for poultry, and fish. And they are the fastest of all composting critters: they can go start to finish in 20 days on new material. They may be one of the ugliest larvae in the business, but they have a lot going for them. They are grown for manure control, animal feed, and use in cosmetics, and, yes, they are edible by man.

The larvae are highly efficient in converting proteins, containing up to 42 percent of protein themselves, plus a lot of calcium and amino acids. Incredibly, in 18 days with adequate feed, 1 gram of black soldier fly eggs turns into 2.4 kilograms of protein-rich larvae. They thus can be a source of protein for animal or human consumption. In a survival situation when all there is to eat is offal, these larvae might start to look pretty good if they can convert that offal to edible matter. In the meantime, you can use them as feed for the fish or fowl you are used to, and only cut out the middleman if you have to in some dark tomorrow.

In 2013 Austrian designer Katharina Unger, peeved at the local meat production establishment, invented a tabletop insect breeding farm called Farm 432, with which folks can produce edible black soldier fly larvae at home in a multichambered plastic machine that looks like a kitchen appliance. According to Unger, "Farm 432 enables people to turn against the

Black soldier fly larvae play a similar role to that of redworms as essential decomposers in breaking down organic substrates and returning nutrients to the soil.

dysfunctional system of current meat production by growing their own protein source." Approximately 500 grams of larvae, or two meals, can be produced in a week by the machine. Unger also notes, "When you cook them, they smell a bit like cooked potatoes. The consistency is a bit harder on the outside and like soft meat on the inside. The taste is nutty and a bit meaty."

Any number of designs of self-contained and even self-harvesting black soldier fly larvae breeding facilities can be built from readily improvised or salvaged inexpensive materials. Working in our favor here is that when the larvae are mature, they head for daylight—a characteristic that can guide them to your hand without the laborious sorting needed for earthworms.

Worm farmers often get transient black soldier fly larvae in their worm bins, but the species do not cohabitate well because active black soldier fly larvae maintain a temperature of up to 100°F, while redworms like it cool. Houseflies avoid facilities with black soldier fly larvae, as they seem to know their own maggots simply cannot compete.

Black soldier fly larvae are best at quickly converting "high-nutrient" waste into animal feed. Redworms are better at converting high-cellulose materials (e.g., paper, cardboard, leaves, non-lignose plant materials) into good compost. Redworms thrive on the residue produced by the fly larvae. Black soldier fly larvae are a superior poultry feed, as they are not known to be intermediate hosts of parasitic worms that infect poultry. Redworms, however, can be host to several.

Although an earthworm can only compete in composting high-cellulose materials, they offer additional benefits, such as soil aeration and, once turned loose, zero maintenance.

All worms are good for our purpose here, as they leave the soil ready for the plants and help maintain the soil as the plant grows. They break down organic matter and make its components available, they naturally adjust the pH as they do so, they aerate and mix the soil as they go up and down to eat or to rest, and they provide a path for surface water to penetrate the soil. There is little not to like about earthworms, unless you want to worry about their methane emissions, but in hard times you can expect hothouse gas generation from other sources to subside dramatically.

Various worms are for sale, but it's been my experience that if you feed them, they will come. And if you feed them well, they will multiply like crazy. The various other creatures—such as centipedes, pill bugs, earwigs, and even slugs—in compost piles are seldom a problem if they are too busy eating mulch to bother your crops.

Both earthworms and black soldier fly larvae should be an integral part of your survival farming protocol; black soldier fly larvae are suitable for direct consumption by man.

Bokashi Bucket

Unless being considered as, or held in reserve for, a protein source, black soldier fly larvae are a little fiddly to grow. Their primary benefits for soil

Close up of earthworm's mouth

building are that they are very fast compared to regular composting and they can directly handle the meat/dairy/fats that you would exclude from your vermicomposting. A middle road to consider is the very simple intermediate step of anaerobic fermentation using bokashi cultures. All the biomass is layered in a sealed bucket with the culture for a couple of weeks; it then is suitable feed for your worm bin or for burying in a compost pile. Worms love the pretreatment; alternatively, when buried, it goes back to soil in only a few more weeks. Bokashi does require one more step, but it is an effortless step—you do have to maintain the culture, which is about like maintaining your favorite sourdough culture. See Chapter 11 on how it also helps to handle human waste.

"Ideal" Compost Isn't Necessary

Purchased rotary composters, labor-intensive compost piles as described above, and other methods at the homesteader or industrial level can work very efficiently, but there are other ways to work with nature to accomplish the same soil building if you'd rather trade more time for less effort.

Passive compost barrel, bin, or heap: A barrel is far more efficient if you cut the bottom out so worms can come up through the soil and break things down for you. A barrel is a little easier to keep the moisture where you like it because the excess can drain out the bottom. A bin or heap lets you more readily turn the pile over for aeration but requires more attention to keeping it moist. "Passive" is the operational term here, so use a heavy poly barrel with holes to admit air, with the bottom cut out. Over a season it will digest several times its volume of feedstock, and at the end of the season or the start of the next season, just knock it over and put it where it is needed or use it to fill growing containers for some other purpose. Or "high-grade" it and screen some for covering newly planted seeds, or leach it in a bucket and use the water as a locally applied tonic to veggies when they have been stressed by weather or are fruiting or flowering.

Composting on the ground: If you mulch heavily with readily biodegradable material—I don't think you can beat lawn trimmings and rabbit manure if you have it— this mulch feeds the worms, soil, and plants, and will really curtail evaporation. Worms will come up to eat the bottom layer and mix and aerate as they do. The whole mass will quickly break down if you keep it moist. Mulch is like petting a cat; there's no such thing as too much. Some commercial compost operations "winrow" compost ingredients on top of the soil, where they are easily turned over with machinery.

Bokashi Bucket

"Composting" in the ground: On a larger scale, one way to build topsoil or rebuild depleted soil is "green manuring." This is simply planting a cover crop in the off season or right after harvest, usually a legume of some sort, which is tilled in while still immature, and it quickly breaks down and is devoured by the worms. If you have access to lots of green biomass and have means to spread or till it, this works ever faster.

Exotic composting: Aside from what nature does every day all over the planet, there exists an art and science of composting far beyond our scope here, and on an industrial level it can be good or bad. The city of Edmonton, Alberta, has built a compost facility the size of several football fields, and it's working. What we used to call a knacker has now gone high-tech and scientifically returns to the soil what began as some really icky stuff, using closed-circuit anaerobic digesters. Yup, composting is a very good thing when done in concert with nature—less so in the case of the buck-a-bag "compost" you buy on sale that is full of wood chips and poison sprays used to kill flies in the feedlot, which will also kill your creeping and crawling gardening buddies, and sometimes even contains residual hostile herbicides that can almost permanently poison your garden plot.

Rotary composter

Fear & Loathing In Fertilizer

SURVIVAL SOMETIMES IS JUST A process of muddling through, never giving up, and eventually persevering just by being the last man standing. More often it is the result of having a plan and being willing to use any resource available and, again, never giving up. In the scenarios addressed here, it is assumed that the natural resources you have available will be subject to being used pretty much as found.

In the context of growing your own food, one resource you will need—and one that you produce yourself, like it or not—is fertilizer. To the Western aesthetic, recycling human waste as fertilizer is a displeasing proposition, but the fact is that in Asia it has always been done and it works quite well, thank you very much, whether I happen to like it or not. As it happens, I don't particularly like the idea, but it works. Since we are trying to think within an arena of high probability, if the methods outlined in this study for generating food work for you, then there is a high probability that sooner or later Dear Reader is going to have to poop. To a Westerner, poo is a liability. To nature and a good portion of humanity on other continents, it is a resource.

Back in the 1950s the City of Olympia, Washington, gave away thoroughly treated sewage sludge as a dry material for landscaping and garden use. The city guaranteed it to be free of every living thing, except tomato seeds. My Uncle Ole's raspberry and leafy-veggie patch was planted in sandy glacial moraine, fertilized with this sludge, lovingly tended, and was a wonder to behold. He also had tomato plants coming up in his lawn. Also in the early 1950s, my father, as an electrical engineer, was involved with an ozone-treatment sewage plant for the City of Longview, Washington. That sewerage product was absolutely sterile, and even toxic metals were inerted as insoluble hydroxides. The Longview Project, as it is known in ozone-oriented circles, was a scientific, but not commercial, success. But you could drink the water.

Now, municipalities have to deal with a plethora of chlorinated hydrocarbons plus undigested/discarded prescription medicines that pass through simple aeration systems. In the event of an infrastructure breakdown, however, there will be no shortage of night soil, and we'll be wishing everybody had a composting toilet. Those city dwellers who never walk on dirt will be unable to dig a slit trench, and in cities it will get ugly real fast. Communal human waste receptacles, of course, are potential breeding grounds and vectors for disease, if disease carrying offal is deposited there and if food crops can come into contact with it.

Humanure

Author/advocate Joseph Jenkins first coined term "humanure" in 1994, but the practice of using human waste as fertilizer is ancient. As is the case with many words that enter the language, it has not yet evolved into a universally precise term, but it does refer to a practice that is eons old. It generally refers to the combination of human feces and urine and associated paper products, plus other carbonaceous material that may be added for composting benefit such as sawdust or straw, which has been thoroughly composted down by processes that ensure it is free of human pathogens. It does not refer to sewerage sludge, which is the omnibus collection from all private and industrial sources, as in a city, nor the biosolids that are often collected at the end of sewage-treatment processes. It does not refer to night soil, which is what you had for dinner yesterday. It is, by any practical or scientific measurement, a suitable soil amendment or fertilizer, cultural or aesthetic shortcomings aside, when properly produced.

The preferable forms of humanure, in descending order of preference, would be the soil from an abandoned old outhouse handily dug up for us by bottle collectors, the product of a modern and properly operated composting toilet, or the composted product of more rustic but effective enterprises as done in parts of the Third World.

Even on the grid with the grid working, there are advantages to a composting toilet. It does not require water or electricity and does not smell when properly managed. It collects human excrement, which is added to a hot compost heap with sawdust, straw, or other carbon-rich materials, where pathogens are destroyed. There it processes the waste in situ, and the nutrients can be returned to the soil. Our diet and waste have high percentages of nitrogen, phosphorus, potassium, carbon, and calcium, equal to or better than those found in (hard-times-unavailable) commercial fertilizer.

Winnow the Poo, from Filth to Tilth

Proper composting of humanure for use on crops would include thermophilic decomposition of the humanure that must heat it sufficiently to destroy harmful pathogens, or enough time must have elapsed since fresh material was added so that biological activity has killed any pathogens. Complete pathogen destruction is assumed at a temperature of 62°C (144°F) for one hour, 50°C (122°F) for one day, 46°C (115°F) for one week, or 43°C (109°F) for one month.

More sophisticated "outhouses" can incorporate manual water systems, be sliver-free hardwood, and be indoors. In these instances capturing the resource for a composting toilet becomes easy.

Many new composting toilets incorporate the use of bokashi cultures, which help eliminate the generation of odor in the toilet and greatly speed the final composting process.

To be safe for crops, a curing stage is often needed to allow a second mesophilic (intermediate temperature) phase to reduce potential phytotoxins (plant poisons). The process that results in humanure kills these pathogens both by the extreme heat of the composting and the extended amount of time (one to two years) that it is allowed to decompose.

Night soil, as distinct from humanure, is best utilized by depositing in a narrow slit trench, deep enough that no insects or vermin will reach it. This, when filled in and covered over, can be a suitable planting bed for top crops, whose roots will reach the humanure. Although many Asian farmers do not make this distinction, it is not suitable for root crops or for surface application.

URINE NO TROUBLE

Depending on diet, urine (chemically quite different than feces) is usually too high in nitrogen or salts for direct application but, when diluted with water, is a premium addition to thick mulch or compost piles. Bedpans have never been one of my favorite things, but in times past communal urinals were used to collect human urine for the defatting of sheep's wool. During the U.S. Civil War, communal deposits of urine and night soil for building niter beds to produce gunpowder were a strategic resource and a civic duty. Since these times, however, the discovery of the microbe and its potentially evil ways has brought such practices into disfavor, at least in the West, where most nitrates are now produced from the 70-percent nitrogen component of the air, via the Haber process.

People excrete far more of certain water-soluble plant nutrients (e.g., nitrogen, phosphorus, potassium) in urine than in feces. Adding a healthy

Composting outdoor open air toilet at Monument Campground on Tonto Hiking Trail in Grand Canyon National Park, Arizona.

In 1820 Europe, folks had to come to grips, so to speak, with night soil because neither municipal sewer systems nor water-flow toilets were in place. The C.W. Steadman lithograph in the Stockholm city museum shows latrinbärerskoror pudrettdamer with a heavily laden skitbärarkärringar.

person's urine to compost usually will increase temperatures and therefore increase its ability to destroy pathogens and unwanted seeds. Urine from a person with no obvious symptoms of infection is generally much more sanitary than fresh feces. Unlike feces, urine doesn't attract disease-spreading flies (such as houseflies or blowflies), and it doesn't contain the more hardy pathogens, such as parasitic worm eggs. Urine usually does not stink for long, particularly when it is fresh, diluted, or put on sorbents, such as straw, sawdust, or mulch.

Urine is primarily composed of water and urea, plus it contains valuable solutes of potassium and phosphorous. Although metabolites of urea are nitrogen fertilizers, it is easy to overfertilize with urine, creating too much ammonia for plants to absorb, acidic conditions, or other plant toxicity. So water it down or pee on the compost.

The E E EWWW-factor of Humanure and Urine

Because various species, including humans, share more diseases in common with their own species than they do with other species, it is usually assumed that animal waste is safer for humans to work with than is human waste. This is an intuitive but not totally accurate assumption because a myriad of diseases—including Maltese fever, chronic wasting disease, mad cow disease, the plague, rabies, Ebola, various influenzas, trichinosis, and various parasites—are common to man and animals and can be passed from one to the other, some through animal waste or carcasses. Even exposure to bat guano can transmit rabies or histoplasmosis through the lungs, or wild rodents can spread the hantavirus. As I write this, international health organizations have concluded that the original victim of the current Ebola outbreak was a little boy who contracted it from a fruit bat being used as bush meat. It is apparently less risky to work with waste from a healthy human than it is with unknown animal waste. It is even less risky to work with your own waste. Since Thomas Crapper popularized the comfortable flush toilet, the waste we produce has become but a fleeting concern in the Western world, and an asset turned into a liability. Like most everybody else, we like to just put the copy of *Field & Stream* back on the water closet, pull the chain, and move on; or in an off-grid situation, take a shovel out to the woods, contemplate the view for a moment, and move on. In a SHTF scenario, however, it is something that must be dealt with. Your individual nest may turn out to be very small, and you do not want to soil a very small nest. In sum: night soil is there and historically useful, and it can be a useful resource— but compost and caveat emptor. You know, I have seen some incredible fruit trees planted over abandoned outhouses.

In the early 20th century, Stockholm had progressed to oilskin and metal containers, hauled by horse carriage men whose job it was to harvest. Yes, they had designated men whose job it was to harvest the streets after the horses. *Photo via Wikipedia*

Modern composting toilets have come a long way since the old days.

Discreet Meat, 'Shrooms

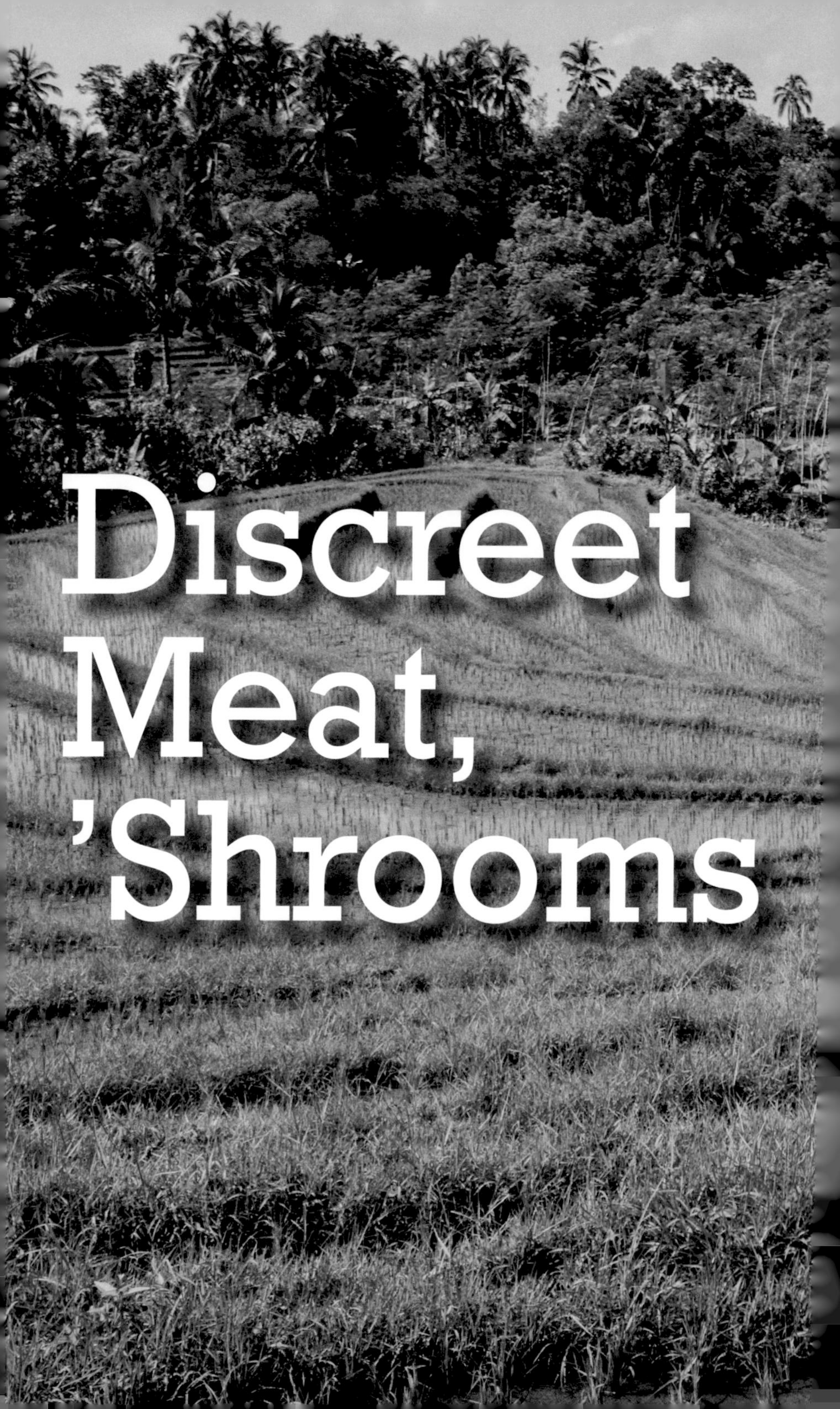

& Fast Food

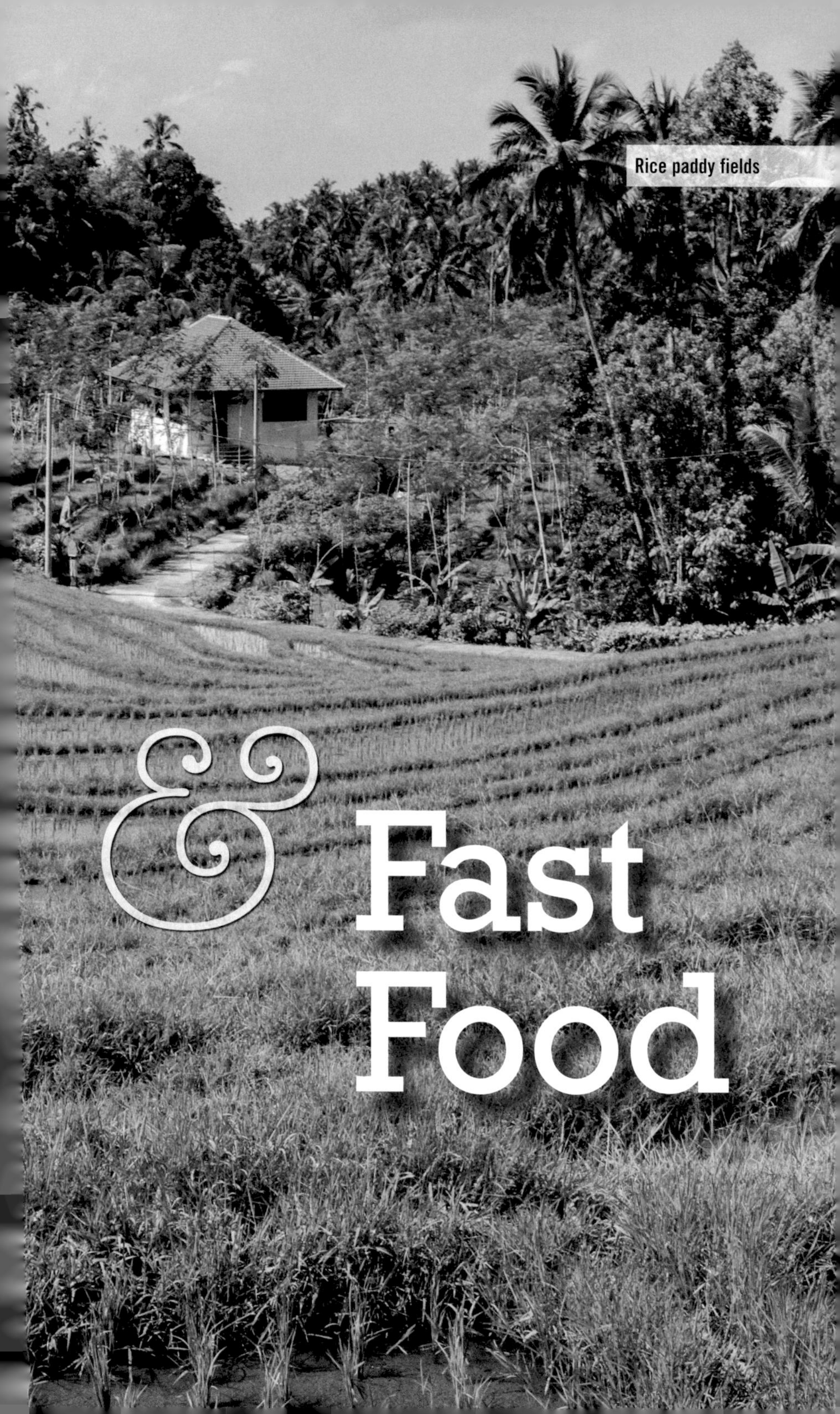

Rice paddy fields

DEPENDING ON WHETHER YOU ARE HANGING OUT or hiding out, your situation may permit raising meat. Obviously, a flock of noisy chickens or a gaggle of honking geese could spell disaster to your low-profile, uninteresting feng shui. But if you have water you might consider Moskovy (quackless) ducks in addition to the bluegill, tilapia, or catfish in your pond. If the situation is appropriate for building cages, I'd probably opt for pigeons (think of them as chickens that eat at the neighbors and then come home to roost, lay eggs, and be harvested), or rabbits (think of them as very quiet chickens that are very easy to harvest: no cluck, no pluck).

If you are situated near a permanent pond, raising "farm" fish or encouraging the growth of native species can be a hassle-free source of protein as well—you can even raise fish in a barrel in the basement.

In this commercial application, an aquaponic system involves tilapia or perch (up to 10,000 fish in the 5-foot-deep tank), watercress, and tomatoes. The water is drawn up through one pump and gravity-fed through the potted plants (which remove the nitrogen from the fish waste) and back into the tank, where it reoxygenizes the tank water. The method can be varied, and the installation can be improvised as long as it has the right elements of design. *Photo: Ryan Griffis, courtesy Growing Power, Milwaukee, Wisconsin.*

Aquaponics: Hydroponics with a meat course

Hydroponics, raising crops in a water solution instead of a soil medium, accounts for a good bit of hothouse-type commercial vegetable production these days, is popular with some home vegetable growers, and has spawned a mini-industry selling "systems," supplies, and paraphernalia to those who follow this course. I readily admit that hydroponics is not my passion, but that art is not covered here only because in a worst-case scenario, the infrastructure, supplies, and paraphernalia required for hydroponic vegetable production will probably not be available. It is in such a situation that I think hands-in-the-dirt techniques will work more reliably.

One intriguing adjunct to hydroponics, however, is the newly rediscovered art usually called aquaponics, wherein effluent from growing fish is used as a hydroponic feedstock, and the plants in turn recondition the water for the fish, like in nature but simplified to produce only what we want to eat.

The Aztecs cultivated chinampas, agricultural islands where plants were raised on stationary (and sometime movable) islands in lake shallows. South China, Thailand, and Indonesia cultivated and farmed rice in paddy fields in combination with fish, and such polycultural farming systems have existed for centuries in many Far Eastern countries, raising such creatures as the oriental loach, swamp eel, common or crucian carp, and pond snails.

The modern art of aquaponics is largely an outgrowth of projects at the New Alchemy Institute and the work of Dr. Mark McMurtry et al. at North Carolina State University. The first aquaponics research in Canada was adjunct to existing aquaculture work at a research station in Lethbridge, Alberta. Canada experienced a surge in aquaponics setups throughout the 1990s, mostly commercial enterprises raising such high-value crops as trout and lettuce. They can be done on a small scale, as part of your self-sufficiency skill set as well.

Plants are grown as in a straight hydroponic system with their roots immersed in the nutrient-rich effluent water from the fish tanks. This enables them to filter out and use the ammonia or its metabolites that is toxic to the aquatic animals. After the water has passed through the hydroponic subsystem, it is cleaned and oxygenated, and can return to the aquaculture vessels. This cycle is continuous. Common aquaponic applications of hydroponic systems vary, but include the following:

- **Deep-water raft aquaponics,** where Styrofoam rafts float in a relatively deep aquaculture basin in troughs.
- **Recirculating aquaponics** (a.k.a. closed-loop aquaponics), where solid media, such as gravel or clay beads, is held in a container that is flooded with water from the aquaculture.
- **Reciprocating aquaponics** (a.k.a. flood-and-drain aquaponics or ebb-and-flow aquaponics), where solid media in a container is alternately flooded and drained utilizing different types of siphon arrangements.

Growing corn
hydroponically

Hydroponic lettuce

Other systems use towers that are trickle-fed from the top, nutrient film technique channels, horizontal PVC pipes with holes for the pots, or plastic barrels cut in half with gravel or rafts in them. Each approach has its own benefits if you are in a situation where you can support them. If you like hydroponic vegetables, there is also a space-saving part of the equation. So if hydroponics is a workable idea for you, it's but a small step up to aquaponics where you get animal protein as well.

Most green leaf vegetables grow well in the hydroponic subsystem of an aquaculture, although the most profitable are varieties of Chinese cabbage, lettuce, basil, roses, tomatoes, okra, cantaloupe, and bell peppers. Other species of vegetables that grow well in an aquaponic system include beans, peas, kohlrabi, watercress, taro, radishes, strawberries, melons, onions,

Growing tomatoes hydroponically

turnips, parsnips, sweet potatoes, and herbs. Since plants at different growth stages require different amounts of minerals and nutrients, plant harvesting is staggered with seedings being grown in with mature plants to ensure stable nutrient content in the water.

Freshwater fish are the most common aquatic animal raised using aquaponics, although freshwater crayfish and prawns are also grown. In practice today, tilapia are the most popular, although exotics such as barramundi, silver perch, eel-tailed catfish or tandanus catfish, jade perch, and Murray cod are also used. For temperate climates, where water temperature is not crucial, bluegill, and catfish are suitable fish species for home systems.

Stock feed usually consists of whatever your particular fish prefer, but do not gear up a system that depends on feed you have to buy. Keep in mind that many fish eat a wide variety of food and that you can probably grow it yourself, from vegetable matter to worms or black soldier fly larvae. Insects are very high in protein, and you may amaze yourself with the quantity you can trap in simple screen-funnel traps with nothing more than a night light as bait. It is not only the commercially promoted turnkey systems that require an intact infrastructure. Although an aquaponic installation could readily be designed and built that is site specific and takes advantage of available wind or waterpower resources, aside from an adequate site, there is a regimen of attention that has to be observed. If you have the location resources and anticipate your being on that site, however, there is a synergism in growing fish that grow your vegetables that may work for you, at least for part of your larder.

Channel catfish

Growing plants with no sunshine

Perhaps one of the best crops to establish in an appropriate setting and then forget is shiitake or other mushrooms grown on rotting logs. All edible mushrooms are high in vitamins and minerals, and most are relatively easy to grow. Most of the common commercial button mushrooms are grown in the dark on composted manure. Check your environs for likely settings to grow 'shrooms. They are tasty and very healthy, preserve well by simple drying, and require minimal care.

Produce in its most efficient form

The earlier assertion that there are crops you can literally grow on your back as you move away from something bad or toward something good only sounds like editorial hyperbole: it's literally true.

This may be the only time I have a chance to use to the old editor's saw about punctuation, illustrated by the headline "Panda Enters Restaurant, Eats, Shoots, and Leaves."

The point here, with apologies, of course, is that you may have to balance the considerations of "eating your seed corn"—never a good idea—eating sprouts now, waiting and eating more leaves, or whether you have time and space to let the particular crop mature to provide a full harvest plus seed for the next planting. Each person's circumstances and resources of time and material will come with infinite variation, but let's outline some of the things to consider.

An old sod house like this one is perfect for growing mushrooms or sprouts.

Sprouts and Greens

Even though it ends the potential for propagation, the sprouting of most seeds changes or enhances their nutritional value. Bean sprouts are an obvious example, but if you have a good supply of seed wheat, wheat sprouts, and grass, they provide a banquet of diverse nutrition compared to the seed as a grain, making them very high in such vitamins as C and A and about as good as it gets for antioxidant content. Alfalfa, although entirely edible as a green, is a favorite macronutritional staple for salads when served up as a sprout. If you're sitting on a stash, for instance, of nitrogen-packed wheat, why not sprout a portion and get the whole and diverse benefit? If you have grown or gleaned some wheat, for instance, but have no way to mill or bake it, simply sprouting it makes it easy to eat and even more nutritious.

Many seeds, including those that can be harvested in the wild, make very nutritious and tasty sprouts—and sprouts are the fastest crop you can grow—or, in some circumstances, may be the only crop you can grow. Growing sprouts in a jar or bag in your backpack may be about the only "gardening" you can do in an extended traveling mode. Many, if not most sprouts, will also do just fine with little or no sunlight, if all you want is the basic sprout (as opposed to, ahem, the more advanced shooting and leaving). Most of the seeds suitable for making sprouts will, if left a bit longer and given some nutritious soil heavy in worm castings, provide substantial greens. Greens, of course, will provide more carbs because they are converting carbon dioxide into starch and sugars, plus added nutritional elements such as chlorophyll.

Beware Commercial Seeds as Food

It is important to note that many seeds grown and marketed for planting, as opposed to human consumption, have been treated to resist rot or mold, repel insects or rodents, and have a longer stable shelf life, among various qualities. Such treatments may only include dusting with a mineral such as powdered dolomite, diatomaceous earth, or borax, but virtually all treatments to resist disease or vermin are highly poisonous to humans, often including heavy metal salts or chlorinated hydrocarbons. A tragic case in point several years back was of a dirt-poor man in Texas who made off with a 100-pound sack of seed wheat to feed his hungry family and whose young daughter suffered severe and permanent central nervous system damage from the heavy metals used to treat this seed, which was not intended to be a foodstuff.

However, natural seeds that have not been treated will sprout into a whole new level of nutrition in almost no time. These include many whose mature plant is not regarded as food and some whose mature plants are simply inedible.

Many groups of "wild" plants have within them varieties that have been domesticated, primarily because they are easy to grow, ship, and market. For instance, in the allium family that includes leeks, onions, and garlic, wild varieties abound. In North America, the long-stemmed wild onions, such as Canada onion or Twincrest onion, provide both edible plants, bulbs, and sprouts, and at seeding time you can grab handfuls of the bulbil or seed heads without even breaking your stride. Feral or naturalized patches, particularly of garlic, are not uncommon around abandoned farmsteads. They're free, they're nutritious, and they sprout.

Especially of interest to someone on the move or without a permanent location are native, wild seeds that are suitable for making edible sprouts. Because there are uncountable wild plants to deal with, making a feeble attempt to catalog those that might have suitable sprouting seeds is beyond the scope of this book. A simple rule of thumb for a best guess might be, if wild birds or rodents are eating the seeds, odds are in your favor the sprouted seed will be edible. But keep in mind that even among the entirely edible seeds and their sprouts, there are caveats. For instance, common domestic black and red beans are toxic to humans in their raw state, so they must be cooked—and so must their sprouts. The same applies, for instance, to wild seeds such as mesquite beans. A premium sprout among sprout aficionados, and a staple pseudo grain in many parts of the world, is the amaranth. These produce small seeds that are a little fiddly to deal with, but they are delicious and nutritious—and common. Various versions of amaranth are mostly known to American farmers as "pig weed" (see "Daily Bread" section in Chapter 1).

Some Good Sprouting Candidates

A wide variety of "sprouting" seeds is commercially available for that purpose, free from chemicals or toxic treatment. Here is a partial list that illustrates the diversity of what is available, including many that are commonly found in the wild or as feral or naturalized plants in areas where there has been earlier human settlement.

- **Alfalfa Sprouts:** Common, easy, delicious; whole plant edible.
- **Alliums:** Garlic, onions, leeks including wild varieties; sprouts from seeds or edible as is bulbils.
- **Almonds:** "Soaks"; just soak them until they swell, don't sprout.
- **Amaranth Sprouts:** Tiny but tasty.
- **Arugula:** Great from sprouts to greens.
- **Beans:** All are good, but black or red beans or their sprouts must be cooked. The most common bean sprout is mung bean, but also suitable are soybeans, turtle beans, adzuki beans, garbanzo beans (a.k.a. chickpeas); many varieties, all good.
- **Broccoli:** Just may be the most nutritious sprout there is.
- **Buckwheat Groat**
- **Cabbage:** All varieties.
- **Carrots**
- **Celery:** Strong microgreens.
- **Chia:** That's right, if your chia pet won't come when you call, eat his hair.
- **Clover:** Sprouts or microgreens; all varieties: red, white.
- **Corn:** All varieties, popcorn a favorite: most are tasty but chewy.
- **Curly Cress:** Excellent microgreens.
- **Daikon**
- **Dill**
- **Fenugreek**
- **Flax (Linseed):** Good microgreens.
- **Grasses:** Rye, wheat, oat, triticale, barley, spelt; as sprouts or juiced.
- **Hazelnut (Filbert):** Just soak like almonds.
- **Hemp Sprouts, Hemp-fiber:** Cannabis is found all over as native or feral plants; seeds/sprouts are virtually devoid of THC.
- **Kale**

- **Kamut**
- **Lemongrass**
- **Lentils:** Red, black.
- **Lettuce**
- **Milk Thistle**
- **Millet**
- **Mizuna**
- **Mustard Greens**
- **Parsley**
- **Peanuts:** Soak and sprout.
- **Peas:** Virtually all.
- **Pumpkin**
- **Quinoa**
- **Radishes:** All varieties, also the fastest crop from seed to maturity.
- **Rice:** All varieties, including wild rice.
- **Sesame**
- **Spinach**
- **Tatsoi:** Tasty microgreens.
- **Turnips**

Only Healthy Sprouts Need Apply

No sprouts in the Solanaceae, or nightshades, family (e.g., tomato, potato, paprikas/pepper, eggplant) can be eaten as sprouts because of the potentially poisonous levels of solanine or other natural toxins. Nor are sprouted rhubarb seeds edible due to toxic levels of oxalic acid. Tomato seeds, not sprouts, are milled for cattle feed but are not for human consumption. Sprouted nuts, such as walnuts or acorns, can contain unhealthy levels of natural toxins as well. The lesson here is that just because part of a plant or seed is edible does not make all the plant edible, nor in all stages of its growth.

Sprouts may be the healthiest form of many edible plants, but bear in mind that the conditions of humidity and temperature that are ideal for a seed to sprout are also ideal for dangerous bacteria to grow. The basic rules are to sprout seeds only from a known source, to wash them before sprouting, and to rinse them frequently with potable water during the sprouting process.

Even commercially grown sprouts have been associated with serious outbreaks of harmful bacteria, including Salmonella and *Escherichia coli* (or *E. coli*). Associated with contaminated seeds or unhygienic production, such outbreaks can be serious, such as a 2011 *E. coli* O104:H4 outbreak in Germany that sickened nearly 4,000 people and killed some 45. It was traced to contaminated mung bean seed from Egypt. One of the most severe *E. coli* outbreaks ever recorded, in Japan in 1996, was associated with radish sprouts. Some 10,000 people, many of them children, fell ill.

Cleanliness and common sense are the best safeguards for small-scale sprouting endeavors. Hobby sprouting is such a worthwhile activity even in normal times that there are many excellent books detailing the best resources for specific seeds and the best practices for sprouting them.

Common causes for sprouts to become contaminated or otherwise inedible include seeds not being rinsed well enough before soaking, seeds being left in standing water after the initial soaking, dirty equipment, insufficient airflow, and a contaminated water source. A poor germination rate may come from seeds that are allowed to dry out or temperatures being too high or too low.

One common thread running through various survival topics is the assumption that a prudent person will have put up, or put into a stash or cache, basic supplies that would otherwise be unavailable in a shortage situation—and in a form that will still be usable when it is retrieved for use. An important point in any stashing/caching exercise is the shelf ife of a given commodity. In this case, it means how long can seeds be stored and still be regarded as viable seeds? Edible seeds can still be edible even if no longer viable, but here we want seeds as seeds.

As a very general rule, seeds of the brassica (cabbage) and legume (bean/pea) families are credited with about five years' shelf life in sealed containers at moderate temperatures, but seeds from various archeological digs dating back 2,000 years have been grown. I have discovered forgotten seed beans that had been in a shed for more than 10 years, and they came up like any others when planted. Most seeds will stay viable exponentially longer if frozen; most seed banks keep the seeds very dry and at about -20°C (just below -0°F). So, the bottom line for sprouting-seed shelf life is to rotate your stock and keep the seeds cool and dry and sealed from oxygen.

Soy bean sprouts

Scenes of societal upheaval like this one from war-torn Sarajevo, Bosnia, inspired the author to write this book about planting and protecting your own food source.

It's All Over but the Sprouting

Whether you are sprouting as a supplement or a crop, on the QT or in the open, the principles are similar over a wide variety of seeds and are readily scaled from a handful to substantial quantities.

The seeds are first rinsed clean of any soil or dirt. Some seeds produce mucilaginous substances when immersed in water, so rinse this off as well. Once rinsed clean, depending on the type and size of seed, they are then soaked for 20 minutes to 12 hours. Soaking increases their water content and wakes them out of their dormant state, or quiescence. They are then rinsed and drained at regular intervals, encouraging them to germinate and sprout.

For small-batch sprouting, the seeds are soaked (big seeds) or moistened (small) and then left at room temperature (13 to 21°C or 55 to 70°F) in an appropriate sprouting vessel. Many types of vessels are commonly used: even a glass jar with cloth or nylon screen fixed over its rim will work fine. Tiered clear-plastic sprouters are available, so different "crops" can be grown at the same time. Any container for sprouting must let water drain away, as immersed sprouts will quickly rot. The seeds swell, may stick to the sides of the jar, and begin germinating within a day or two.

Sprouts are rinsed two to four times a day, depending on the climate and type of seed, to provide moisture and prevent their souring. Each seed has its own ideal sprouting time. After three to five days, most sprouts will have grown to 2–3 inches long and will be suitable for consumption. Many species can be left longer to develop leaves and are then known as baby greens. A popular baby green is sunflower after 7–10 days. Refrigeration can be used if available to slow or halt the growth of sprouts.

If you are new to sprouting, mung beans provide a good test run. They can be sprouted in light or dark conditions. Those germinated in the dark will be crisper and whiter, but they are more nutritious if grown in partial sunlight (full sunlight is not recommended because it can cause the beans to overheat or dry out).

An efficient way to sprout such beans as lentils or azuki is in a colander. Soak the beans in water for about 8 hours and then place in the colander; rinse well twice a day. Sprouting is also applied on a large scale to barley as a part of the malting process for making beer, or to corn for making whiskey. You probably knew that, but keep in mind that the distinctive aroma of malting grains can give you away.

Sprouting and Sprinting

This kind of "gardening on the move" is readily accomplished on any scale from a container hanging on your backpack to several dedicated shelves in your Winnebago.

Getting started:

There Is No Better Time Than Now

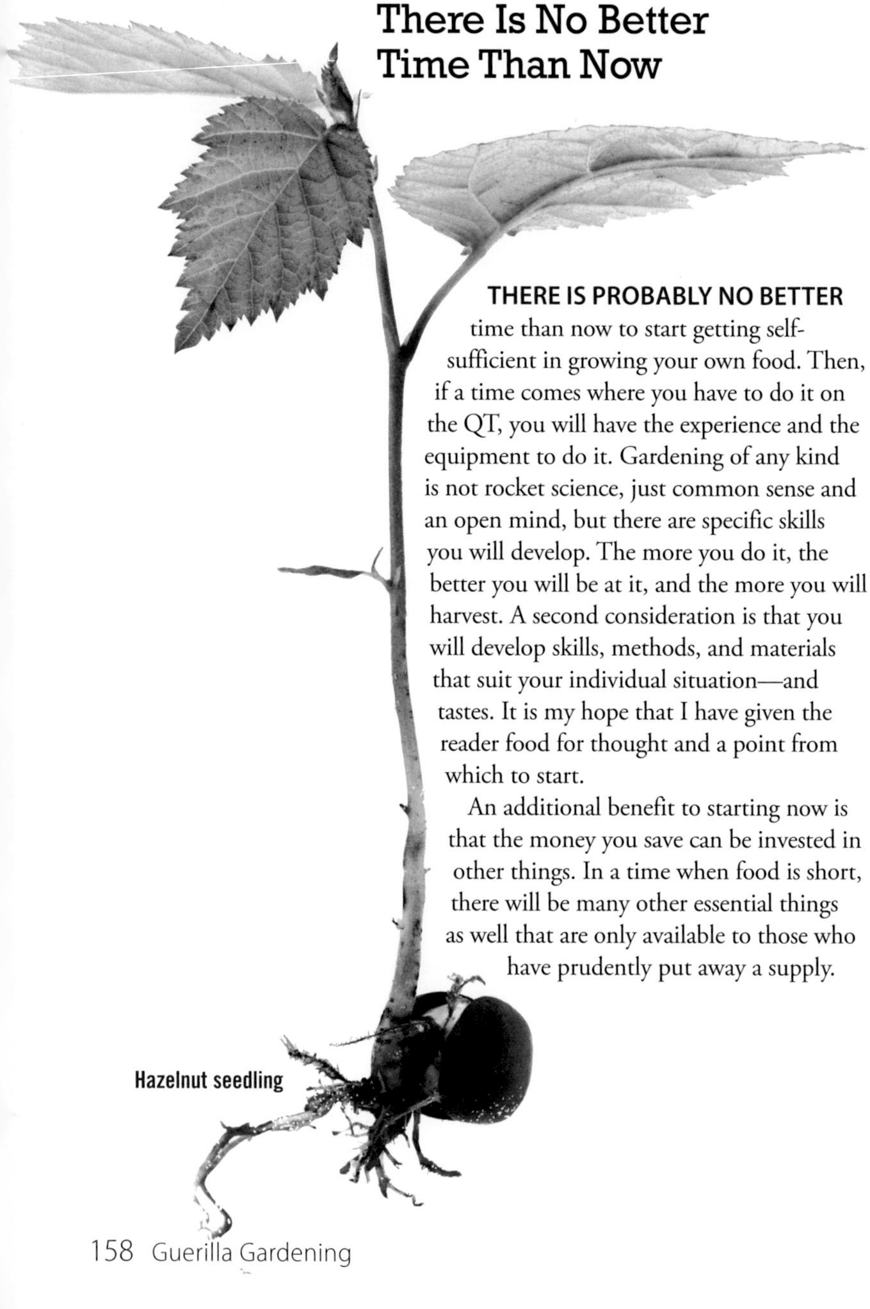

THERE IS PROBABLY NO BETTER time than now to start getting self-sufficient in growing your own food. Then, if a time comes where you have to do it on the QT, you will have the experience and the equipment to do it. Gardening of any kind is not rocket science, just common sense and an open mind, but there are specific skills you will develop. The more you do it, the better you will be at it, and the more you will harvest. A second consideration is that you will develop skills, methods, and materials that suit your individual situation—and tastes. It is my hope that I have given the reader food for thought and a point from which to start.

An additional benefit to starting now is that the money you save can be invested in other things. In a time when food is short, there will be many other essential things as well that are only available to those who have prudently put away a supply.

Hazelnut seedling

Field Notes:

Field Notes

Field Notes